Exploring **C**anada

THE MARITIME PROVINCES

by Gordon D. Laws and Lauren M. Laws

LUCENT
BOOKS®

THOMSON

———— ✦ ————™

GALE

San Diego • Detroit • New York • San Francisco • Cleveland • New Haven, Conn. • Waterville, Maine • London • Munich

Development, management, design, and composition by Pre-Press Company, Inc.

LIBRARY OF CONGRESS CATALOGING-IN-PUBLICATION DATA

Laws, Gordon D.
  The Maritime Provinces / by Gordon D. Laws and Lauren M. Laws.
     p. cm. — (Exploring Canada)
Summary: Examines the history, geography, climate, industries, people,
and culture of Canada's Maritime Provinces.
Includes bibliographical references and index.
  ISBN 1-59018-335-5 (hardback : alk. paper)
  1. Maritime Provinces--Juvenile literature. [1. Maritime Provinces. 2.
Canada.] I. Laws, Lauren M. II. Title. III. Exploring Canada (Lucent
Books)
  F1035.8.L39 2004
  971.5--dc21

                                         2003005440

Contents

Foreword

Any truly accurate portrait of Canada would have to be painted in sharp contrasts, for this is a long-inhabited but only recently settled land. It is a vast and expansive region peopled by a predominantly urban population. Canada is also a nation of natives and immigrants that, as its Prime Minister Lester Pearson remarked in the late 1960s, has "not yet found a Canadian soul except in time of war." Perhaps it is in these very contrasts that this elusive national identity is waiting to be found.

Canada as an inhabited place is among the oldest in the Western Hemisphere, having accepted prehistoric migrants more than eleven thousand years ago after they crossed a land bridge where the Bering Strait now separates Alaska from Siberia. Canada is also the site of the New World's earliest European settlement, L'Anse aux Meadows on the northern tip of Newfoundland Island. A band of Vikings lived there briefly some five hundred years before Columbus reached the West Indies in 1492.

Yet as a nation Canada is still a relative youngster on the world scene. It gained its independence almost a century after the American Revolution and half a century after the wave of nationalist uprisings in South America. Canada did not include Newfoundland until 1949 and could not amend its own constitution without approval from the British Parliament until 1982. "The Sleeping Giant," as Canada is sometimes known, came within a whisker of losing a province in 1995, when the people of Quebec narrowly voted down an independence referendum. In 1999 Canada carved out a new territory, Nunavut, which has a population equal to that of Key West, Florida, spread over an area the size of Alaska and California combined.

As the second largest country in the world (after Russia), the land itself is also famously diverse. British Columbia's "Pocket Desert" near the town of Osoyoos is the northernmost desert in North America. A few hundred miles away, in Alberta's Banff National Park, one can walk on the Columbia Icefields, the largest nonpolar icecap in the world. In parts of Manitoba and the Yukon, glacially created sand dunes creep slowly across the landscape. Quebec and Ontario have so many lakes in the boundless north that tens of thousands remain unnamed.

One can only marvel at a place where the contrasts range from the profound (the first medical use of insulin) to the mundane (the invention of Trivial Pursuit); the sublime (the poetry of Ontario-born Robertson Davies) to the ridiculous (the comic antics of Ontario-born Jim Carrey); the British (ever-so-quaint Victoria) to the French (Montreal, the world's second-largest French-speaking city); and the environmental (Greenpeace was founded in Vancouver) to the industrial (refuse from nickel mining near Sudbury, Ontario, left a landscape so barren that American astronauts used it to train for their moon walks).

Given these contrasts and conflicts, can this national experiment known as Canada survive? Or to put it another way, what is it that unites as Canadians the elderly Inuit woman selling native crafts in the Yukon; the millionaire businessman-turned-restaurateur recently emigrated from Hong Kong to Vancouver; the mixed-French (Métis) teenager living in a rural settlement in Manitoba; the cosmopolitan French-speaking professor of archaeology in Quebec City; and the raw-boned Nova Scotia fisherman struggling to make a living? These are questions only Canadians can answer, and perhaps will have to face for many decades.

A true portrait of Canada cannot, therefore, be provided by a brief essay, any more than a snapshot captures the entire life of a centenarian. But the Exploring Canada series can offer an illuminating overview of individual provinces and territories. Each book smartly summarizes an area's geography, history, arts and culture, daily life, and contemporary issues. Read individually or as a series, they show that what Canadians undeniably have in common is a shared heritage as people who came, whether in past millennia or last year, to a land with a difficult climate and a challenging geography, yet somehow survived and worked with one another to form a vibrant whole.

Atlantic Canada

The maritime provinces of New Brunswick, Nova Scotia, and Prince Edward Island lie on Canada's eastern seaboard and comprise some of the most beautiful coastal land in the hemisphere. The land is a striking mixture of features—towering rock formations and forest-covered mountains in New Brunswick, a saltwater lake and glacier-carved river valleys in Nova Scotia, and gently rolling hills and picturesque dunes on Prince Edward Island. "The Maritime Provinces of Canada form a region of surprise," says travel writer Harry Bruce. "There is still room for them. Its history is full of French-English warfare, privateers, and shipwrecks, but it has languished economically. The population (still under two million) has therefore never been big enough to obliterate the wilderness or deface the immensely intricate 5,200-mile coastline."[1]

In all three provinces, the sea is a paramount feature. The sea moderates the cold but also produces heavy fogs, higher rain totals than inland areas, and brisk winds. For centuries the lifestyles of the people have been dictated by the sea, and the people have enjoyed the benefits of the land. The early native peoples, the Mi'kmaq and the Maliseet, thrived on cyclical periods of fishing the seas and rivers and hunting in the forests. The plentiful woodlands and fertile valleys provided large game and sufficient plants for shelter and food. The coming Europeans found the Maliseet and Mi'kmaq to be adept at use of the land and skillful traders. Though difficulties later followed, Europeans learned to rely on the resources the natives had always enjoyed.

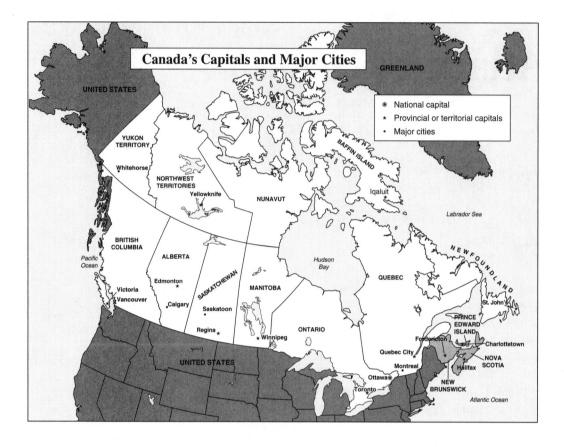

Advances in technology increased the maritimes' importance over the years. Seemingly endless numbers of fish could be caught, and expansive forests could be harvested for shipbuilding and the lumber trade. The provinces were, for a time, pillars in early Canada. Charlottetown, Prince Edward Island's capital city, was the site of a landmark 1864 independence conference, and three years later Nova Scotia and New Brunswick became two of the first four original provinces in the new country of Canada. But the reliance on resources that proved ultimately to be limited posed a grave challenge as the world economy evolved in new directions. During much of the twentieth century, population growth in the maritimes was stagnant, economies stumbled along, and education and health services suffered.

Even so, the striking natural beauty of the provinces and the feeling of isolation from the rest of the mainland gave residents a distinct character. Generations loved the sea and cherished their independence from mainland Canada. When progress and development finally began to arrive, many maritimers were reluctant to sacrifice the simple lifestyles and independence they had enjoyed.

New Directions

Today, the provinces are charging into a new era of unprecedented prosperity and economic growth. While the overall success of the provinces has long been tied to trading and to volatile industries, such as fishing and forestry, that led to boom-and-bust economic cycles, today's political leaders are successfully diversifying the economies into fields such as communications and high technology. Tourism has also exploded as visitors arrive to see the many unique and spectacular natural attractions in the maritimes. Among these are one of the deepest natural harbors in the world (Halifax), tides in the Bay of Fundy that are some of the highest in the world (and that create the famous "Reversing Falls" of the Saint John River), and sandy beaches on Prince Edward Island that are tinted red by iron oxide.

■ A twice-daily high tide causes the Saint John River to flow upstream at Reversing Falls.

Within recent years the maritime provinces' historically high unemployment rates have gradually come down, even while much of the rest of Canada muddles along through the global recession. Further, innovations in the fishing trade, and a new appreciation for conservation, have helped to revive this central sector of the regional economy. The economic successes have been accompanied by improvements in social services, such as health care and education. Even the language tensions that divide Quebec are largely absent from maritime politics—the large French contingent in New Brunswick has access to French schools, radio, and television.

The provinces are working today to secure the foundations for the future. The needs of the economy sometimes conflict with environmental or social issues, and rising health care costs are a major concern since the population, on average, is aging. In addition, many people are reluctant to let the traditional lifestyles embraced by many maritimers get swept away by the new demands of fast-paced industrial society. Balancing these conflicting needs and desires promises to be an ongoing challenge.

Bound by the Sea

New Brunswick, Nova Scotia, and Prince Edward Island are collectively called the maritimes or, with Newfoundland included, the Atlantic provinces. The maritimes lie on the eastern seaboard of Canada, just north and east of Maine in the United States. In many ways, they are united, sharing a common climate and locale. In particular, the three provinces share the sea. The Atlantic Ocean and the Gulf of St. Lawrence dictate much of the climate and have had important effects on the land formations and the lives of the people. Further, the sea holds vast resources, from deep harbors to fish to natural gas and oil reserves.

Despite the similarities, the provinces are different—strikingly in many places. While Nova Scotia and New Brunswick are formed out of rock and lava foundations, Prince Edward Island is essentially a large deposit of sand and sediment. Even New Brunswick and Nova Scotia differ vastly in their natural offerings, their tree-covered areas, and their resources. The weather, the land, and the resource challenges can be difficult, but these features give the provinces their distinct characters.

The Shapes of the Provinces

The maritime provinces differ vastly in size, shape, and geological formation. New Brunswick is the land channel to the rest of the continent for the three provinces. It is 28,355 square miles (73,440 square kilometers) in total area, about the size of Maine, the state that bounds New Brunswick to the south. The province is also bounded by Quebec's Gaspé Peninsula to the west. The eight-mile- (thirteen-kilometer) long Confederation Bridge, completed in 1997, crosses the

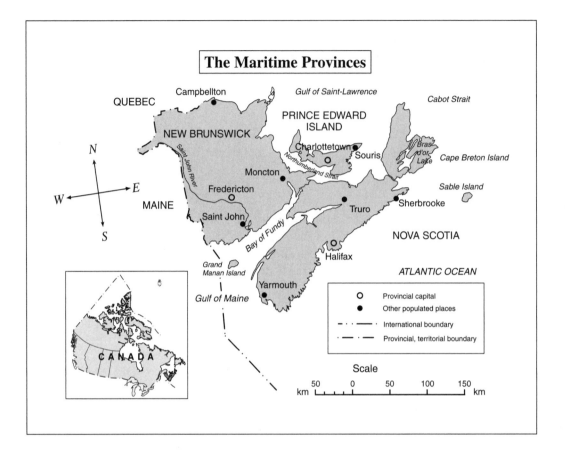

The Maritime Provinces

Northumberland Strait and links New Brunswick to Prince Edward Island.

By contrast, Nova Scotia, to New Brunswick's east, is more seabound even than New Brunswick. "Nova Scotia extends like a long foot into the Atlantic," notes *Smithsonian* writer Mary Duenwald, "connected to New Brunswick by a thin ankle."[2] Nova Scotia is linked to New Brunswick by the Chignecto Isthmus, a stretch of land only 15 miles (27 kilometers) wide at its narrowest. Nova Scotia's land area is about three-quarters of New Brunswick's and includes almost 5,000 miles (8,000 kilometers) of coastline. At its widest point Nova Scotia is no broader than 80 miles (130 kilometers). Thus, every major population center is just a short distance from the sea, and the sea's effect on the people is profound.

Prince Edward Island is perhaps the most distinct of the three provinces. Smaller than the state of Delaware, it is also the smallest Canadian province, making up only 0.1 percent of the country's total land area. Prince Edward Island is not even the largest island in the maritime provinces: Nova Scotia's Cape Breton Island is about twice its size. Crescent-shaped Prince Edward Island stretches a mere 139 miles (224 kilometers) end to end, with widths ranging from about 3 to 37 miles (4 to 60 kilometers). But the stunning beauty of the island and its fertile land have always attracted settlers and visitors. Today, the island has the highest concentration of people among the provinces and territories, with 62 people per square mile (24 people per square kilometer). That population swells five-fold during the summer when tourists flock to the island for its beaches and its hiking- and biking-friendly landscape of gently rolling hills.

Distinctive Land Features

New Brunswick and Nova Scotia lie atop a 500-million-year-old rock foundation that runs from the southeastern United States up through Newfoundland. Ancient lava flows left large

■ *Biking the back roads of Prince Edward Island is a favorite summertime activity.*

■ Nova Scotia: Warden of the North

The vaguely lobster-like shape of Nova Scotia and its relationship with the sea are key characteristics that shaped everyday life over centuries in Nova Scotia. Nova Scotia's land is a natural defense against invasion from the east. Thus, Halifax, its capital city, has over the years been the scene of numerous military battles.

Further, Nova Scotia has deep natural harbors, unlike Prince Edward Island (which has virtually none) and New Brunswick (which has only a few). These deep natural harbors opened Nova Scotia to settlement and commercial shipping, but also left it vulnerable to privateering. Nova Scotia's harbors have been a launching point for daring sea rescues. A number of the survivors of the ill-fated *Titanic* were rescued by ships launched from Nova Scotia.

Today, Nova Scotia's unique shape and coastal location make it a natural playground for tourists. Hiking trails extend—some treacherously—along the spectacular coasts. Whale tour boats launch from Nova Scotia's shores, and residents enjoy much of the culinary goodness the sea has to offer.

deposits of lead, copper, and zinc in the northwestern corner of New Brunswick. The central and eastern sections of New Brunswick include coal-rich sandstones, while other parts of the province contain salt and oil deposits.

The low hills of Nova Scotia are less rugged than New Brunswick's mountains. Fertile valleys like Annapolis and Cornwallis were left behind when inland seas receded and deposited sediments. Glaciers also carved valleys and rivers. The deposits of gypsum, limestone, coal, and salt, as well as offshore oil and natural gas, are mainstays of the current economy.

Prince Edward Island is quite distinct from its sister provinces in its landforms. Streams in ancient highlands drained sediments into a bed in the present-day Gulf of Lawrence. Glaciers covered this vast area of sedimentary land about seventy-five thousand years ago. The weight of the glaciers depressed and scoured much of the landscape. As the glaciers melted and receded roughly ten thousand years ago, some of the land rose. With the weight of the glaciers removed, a low-lying plain surfaced to connect the island to the mainland. Later, a crescent-shaped piece of land, today's island, formed. Much of the sediment left behind is rich in iron, giving the province's land its distinctive reddish tint. Fortunately for farmers, the sediments are fertile.

Stony Mountains and Fertile Valleys

New Brunswick has two main geographical regions: the north and east coasts, and the Bay of Fundy and Saint John River valley in the south. The northernmost section of New Brunswick is made up of uplands and small mountains. The tallest mountain, Mount Carleton, rises to 2,690 feet (820 meters), the highest point in the maritime provinces. The uplands give way to rolling, wooded hills in the center and eastern portions of the province. These hills served as natural barriers during early settlement, so that the largely French communities of the northern and eastern coasts are distinct from the mainly British communities in the south. The province's southern region is made up of craggy hills that descend into tidal marshes and lowland plains.

New Brunswick's land is generally unfriendly to farming. Barely 5 percent of the province is agricultural land, with much of the most fertile area lying along the Saint John River. More than 80 percent of the land is wooded. Virtually all of the woodland is good for forestry—spruce, fir, cedar, and pine are some of the softwood trees that make up 45 percent of the forestland. Maple, poplar, birch, and oak trees are just a few of the hardwoods that make up 27 percent of the forestland. The remaining forestland is mixed. Many of the forestlands are marshy or swampy, and such areas support moss, lichens, ferns, and cranberries.

Nova Scotia, in contrast, offers somewhat larger stretches of agricultural land. Still, Nova Scotia's agricultural land is relatively small—just 10 percent of the total area—and is generally confined to valleys and lowlands. The lowlands near the Bay of Fundy, which separates western Nova Scotia from eastern New Brunswick, and Northumberland Strait are particularly good agricultural regions because the high tides create marshland. Dikes built in these marshlands drain the standing water and leave behind soil rich in minerals and nutrients.

Much of Nova Scotia is stony uplands with soils that are thin and acidic. The highest point in Nova Scotia is White Hill, a peak on Cape Breton Island that is 1,745 feet (532 meters) high. While White Hill is treeless, much of Cape Breton Island is not. Most of the forests that covered Nova Scotia before European settlement have been stripped, except on Cape Breton where a lot of good forestland remains. Even so, coniferous trees are most common in the mountains and uplands, and hardwoods like maple and birch persist. Like

New Brunswick, Nova Scotia has many low-lying bogs and marshes along the coasts. Colorful wildflowers like mayflowers, water lilies, and violets are common in milder regions, and cranberries, blueberries, and goldenrod thrive all over the province.

An Island of Lowlands

While mountains and rolling hills dot the other two provinces, Prince Edward Island is generally low-lying. The western edge of the island is entirely flat, but gentle hills poke up from the middle of the island before subsiding in the east. The highest point on Prince Edward Island is a mere 466 feet (142 meters) above sea level.

■ *Prince Edward Island National Park features red sandstone cliffs as well as some of Canada's longest and most popular beaches.*

■ Elephant Rock Fading Away

Near the village of Norway on the northwestern shore of Prince Edward Island is Elephant Rock, a massive sandstone formation sitting in the water just off the beach. Originally a section of high coastal bluff, through erosion the reddish rock became detached and now stands alone in the sea. Its sixty-six-foot- (twenty-meter) high cliffs are some of the steepest in the province, and its distinctive red appearance reminds visitors of the unique soil and land formation of Prince Edward Island.

Elephant Rock takes its name from its remarkable similarity to the shape of an elephant. Today, however, it is not quite as elephant-like as it once was. That is because in 1998 the eroded pillar of rock running from the bluff to the sea, which formed the elephant's "trunk," collapsed into the water during a winter storm. "It looked so much like an elephant. I guess it really did come alive," area resident Jo-Anne Wallace lamented to *The Guardian,* a Charlottetown paper. "People would come two or three times every summer to look at it. They had been there before and they'd go again. I did it myself. . . . It was part of us, part of West Prince, part of Prince Edward Island."

Area residents feared that Elephant Rock's sad erosion would have a disastrous effect on the sleepy West Prince area's small tourism industry, since Elephant Rock was the area's major attraction, sometimes drawing five thousand visitors a week during the summer. Local officials have said that some other type of ecotourism attraction, such as boardwalks through the local bogs, might eventually replace the elephant. In *Canada's Maritime Provinces,* travel writer David Stanley agrees, noting that "it's still a hauntingly beautiful, almost desolate place, and you feel you've really reached the end of Prince Edward Island."

The island's shores are famous for their striking beauty. They alternate between steep sandstone bluffs and long sandy beaches. The north shore of the island is notable for extensive formations of sand dunes and deep tidal inlets. The interior of Prince Edward Island is much more amenable to agriculture than is the land of New Brunswick and Nova Scotia, and most spots on the island can produce crops. More than 50 percent of the land is considered "highly productive," and 90 percent of the land is suitable for at least some type of agriculture. Among the major crops grown are potatoes (the province is sometimes called "spud island") and tobacco.

Prince Edward Island once harbored upland stretches of forest with beech, maple, oak, and pine trees. Over the past century most of these woodlands have disappeared due to fire, disease, and logging. Efforts are under way to protect and expand some of the island's remaining forests, mostly a mix of spruce, balsam fir, and red maple.

Prince Edward Island has fewer valuable natural resources compared to the other two maritime provinces. The rivers lack dramatic falls so the province has to rely on fossil fuels rather than hydroelectric power for its energy needs. Fresh water is in relatively low supply. Trace amounts of coal and uranium exist in some areas, and natural gas has been discovered off of the northeast coast of the province, but so far these finds have not proven to be commercially viable.

The Offshore Environment

While the landforms have been key factors in the lives of maritime residents, none have been as important as the sea. Even in the farthest corner of New Brunswick, residents are only a half-day's drive from the sea. Fishing has long been a key industry for all three provinces. Lobster, crab, herring, and cod have generally been the most important sea creatures caught along the coasts of the three provinces. In the early 1990s, overfishing of cod resulted in a ban on commercial cod fishing, but the fishery remains strong for all three provinces. The sea also yields important shellfish like scallops, oysters, clams, and mussels.

The sea physically shapes the dramatic coastal environments. Nova Scotia's coastline is jagged, marked by inlets, coves, and bays. The province has some four thousand coastal islands along its shores, adding to the striking shoreline features. Further, the tides in the Bay of Fundy are world-renowned. In a narrow stretch of the bay, for about 150 miles (240 kilometers) high tide forces water forward and causes it to reach heights of 52 feet (16 meters) above low-tide marks. These high tides allow the loading of lumber and other products for shipment around the world. Prince Edward Island's coastline is marked by tidal inlets. The coast is shifty, and sand deposits in the north can clog harbor entrances and keep fishermen from docking. In New Brunswick, the Bay of Fundy region has many inlets and natural harbors that are important for shipping and for the fishing industry.

At least for Nova Scotia, the seas could prove potentially profitable in other resources. The maritimes' most promising stores of oil and gas appear off of Nova Scotia's Sable Island, a

sandy island that sits more than 100 miles (170 kilometers) out to sea and is the only above-water portion of the outer continental shelf near the provinces. Exploratory drilling continues along the shores of all three provinces.

■ *The Bay of Fundy's dramatic tidal swings can temporarily ground ships, like the one shown in this photo from the 1860s.*

Abundant Rivers and Lakes

While Prince Edward Island is marked with only a handful of ponds and small rivers, glacier-carved and ocean-formed rivers and lakes are important features of Nova Scotia and New Brunswick. Nova Scotia alone has more than three thousand lakes, formed in part because of the irregular shape of the uplands, glaciers that receded and left deposits of water, and high seas that covered lands, then receded. There are also hundreds of rivers and streams in Nova Scotia, though most are short because of the direction and shapes of the lakes.

The maritimes' largest lake is Nova Scotia's Bras d'Or at 425 square miles (1,100 square kilometers). It was created when the ocean flooded over an area of Cape Breton Island between upland and lowland areas. Today the saltwater lake is widely used for recreation. The largest lake on the peninsula of Nova Scotia is Lake Rossignol, which is also the largest freshwater lake in the maritime provinces. Located in southern Nova Scotia, the lake area is an important habitat for

■ *An angler fishes for trout on Prince Edward Island's Wheatley River.*

birds and animals. The numerous short rivers of the province have historically been important for transporting goods to the sea.

In New Brunswick, the rivers offer access to the few fertile regions. The Saint John River is the most important inland water source for New Brunswick. Almost 400 miles (670 kilometers) long, it originates in Maine and forms part of the border between the United States and Canada. Where the river cradles the city of Saint John, the Bay of Fundy's tides regularly drive it back through a narrow gorge called Reversing Falls. Several hydroelectric stations along the Saint John River provide much of the province's energy needs. While the Saint John is New Brunswick's most important river, other rivers and tributaries provide vital connections to the ocean and help move timber and resources to shipping channels. The lakes in the province are a source of both recreation and fishing—trout, salmon, pickerel, and bass are caught frequently in lakes. The largest lake, Grand Lake, is fed by the Saint John River and is notable for the beautiful views from its varied shoreline, including three large coves.

Prince Edward Island differs significantly from its sister provinces in inland water. There are more than 2,485 miles (4,000 kilometers) of streams, and though many are called rivers—Mill River, Wheatley, and others—they are generally estuaries (streams that are a mix of freshwater and saltwater). Few natural lakes dot the island (Glenfinnan and O'Keefe lakes being the notable exceptions), but over the years, residents have dammed water and created more than eight hundred freshwater ponds. The rivers and lakes do not serve any significant amounts of shipping, but they are good for fishing. Virtually all streams have fish, particularly trout, and many of the estuaries, such as the Morell River on the northeastern side of the island, are home to salmon.

Varied Wildlife Across Varied Lands

The forests and fertile valleys of the maritime provinces are home to numerous wildlife species common to southern Canada. Notable birds and animals include snowy owl, bald eagle, beaver, porcupine, snowshoe hare, fox, white-tailed deer, and black bear. The moose is the largest land animal in the region and can be found in forests of the provinces.

■ *Bald eagles breed on Cape Breton Island and numerous other places throughout the maritime provinces.*

■ Where Whales Frolic

Among the best places in the maritime provinces to see whales are where the Bay of Fundy meets the Gulf of Maine, and in the Cabot Strait north of Cape Breton. Whale-spotting tours launch from the Fundy Isles in New Brunswick and from Brier Island off the tip of Digby Neck, a long peninsula in southwest Nova Scotia. Tours also operate out of Ingonish, Pleasant Bay, and other ports on Cape Breton. So plentiful are the whales that boat captains offer either a money-back guarantee that tourists will see whales or a raincheck to go out later.

The most commonly viewed whales are sixty-foot- (twenty-one meter) long finbacks, with the smaller humpbacks and minke whales not far behind. The endangered right whale, which can weigh up to sixty tons, is seen more rarely. Of these species, the humpback is the most dazzling to watch, breaching above the water's surface while flapping the flukes of their tails. Humpbacks send up crowd-pleasing splashes as they crash back into the sea. Smaller whale species such as pilot whales and killer whales (orca) are occasionally spotted off of Cape Breton.

While the whales are the stars of any tour, the waters are also full of porpoises, dolphins, and seals. Bald eagles are sometimes seen soaring overhead.

■ *A humback whale's tail pushes out of the water in Cabot Strait.*

Various species have adapted to important land characteristics of the provinces and thus diversify the wildlife found in the maritimes. Nova Scotia hosts more than 440 species of bird. Sandpipers nest and live in the mudflats, while great blue herons can be found along the shorelines. Common terns nest on Nova Scotia beaches and islands in large colonies that provide defense for the flocks as a whole. Most notably, Nova Scotia is home to the largest bald eagle population east of the Rocky Mountains.

All three provinces host important endangered species. The endangered piping plover nests on sandy beaches along the north shore of Prince Edward Island, the west coast of New Brunswick, and the southwest end of Nova Scotia. A migratory bird, the plover heads to Florida and the Caribbean for the winter, but stays much of the rest of the year in the provinces.

The offshore environment of the maritime provinces provides a home not only to fish but to the mammoths of the deep—whales. Finback, humpback, and minke whales frequent the plankton-rich coastal waters of the maritime provinces from July to October.

A Climate Tempered by the Sea

As with most other aspects of life in the maritimes, the climate is greatly affected by the ocean. Like New England, the maritimes have four distinct seasons of more or less the same length. The warmest summer months are mild. For example, average daily highs in Halifax and Saint John during July and August are in the low 70s F (low 20s C). Neither city has ever experienced a truly scorching day—record highs are 90° F (32°C) for Halifax and 91°F (33°C) for Saint John—because of the effect of cooling ocean breezes.

The Atlantic also has a slight moderating effect on the winter, though it remains long, cold, and pregnant with rain, fog, and snow. In January, average daily lows drop to 9°F (−13°C) in Saint John and even lower in points north, such as Bathhurst. Halifax and other coastal communities enjoy slightly higher winter temperatures. Nova Scotia even has a small group of dedicated winter surfers—wetsuits required, of course.

Rain and snow in the provinces are plentiful, and the ocean also causes considerable fog in the coastal areas. While Fredericton, N.B., and Charlottetown, P.E.I., average a damp three to four inches (eight to ten centimeters) of precipitation each

■ *Foggy weather is common in the fishing village of Peggy's Cove, Nova Scotia, which is famous for its picturesque harbor.*

month, Saint John averages four to six inches (ten to fifteen centimeters). Kept cooler than most areas in the summer by ocean breezes, Halifax also experiences more rain throughout the year. The number of wet days in Halifax ranges from fourteen in September to twenty-five in December and January.

Dwellers by the Sea

The ocean's natural beauty, abundant wildlife, and moderating effect on climate have brought people to the maritime regions for thousands of years. Before the arrival of Europeans, native peoples thrived on the sea's bounty. European settlers learned from the natives and the two groups remain closely connected to the seas today.

Native Peoples and European Settlers

R esidents of the maritime provinces have long relied on the ocean and the land's natural resources for survival. The original natives ("First Nations") lived for thousands of years in this region before the coming of the Europeans. The maritimes were attractive to early explorers and settlers primarily because of the resources that native peoples had discovered so long ago—fertile soil on Prince Edward Island, convenient water routes on Nova Scotia and New Brunswick, and vast timber and fish resources.

The Mi'kmaq and the Maliseet

The main First Nations in the maritime region were the Mi'kmaq (also known as Micmac) and Maliseet (Malecite). They spoke versions of an Algonquian language and belonged to a larger body of eastern woodlands tribes. The Mi'kmaq generally occupied areas east of the Saint John River in New Brunswick and various parts of Nova Scotia and Prince Edward Island. The Maliseet occupied areas west of the Saint John River in New Brunswick and Maine.

For centuries, the Mi'kmaq called themselves L'nu'k, which simply means "the people" or "human beings." Their present name comes from the native word *nikmaq,* meaning "my kin-friends." The Maliseet closely identified themselves with the Saint John River—they called themselves Welustuk, "of the beautiful river."

The early history of these peoples is somewhat unclear. Evidence on Prince Edward Island suggests that Mi'kmaq ancestors were living there as early as ten thousand years ago. These original peoples may have made their way to Prince Edward Island by crossing a low plain now covered by the Northumberland Strait. Native occupation in other parts of the maritimes has extended back for thousands of years. By the time Europeans encountered them, these eastern tribes had developed complex societies rich in artistic, spiritual, and social practices.

Mi'kmaq Settlements and Lifestyle

Mi'kmaq settlements were typically made up of individual or joint households clustered on a bay or a river. The Mi'kmaq lived in wigwams (*wikuom*, in the native language, a dwelling), large structures made of lashed poles covered by birch bark and capable of housing twelve to fifteen people. Clothes were made from the skins of animals and were tanned with animal brains, bird livers and oil, and smoke. The Mi'kmaq traveled in birch bark canoes up to twenty-five feet (eight meters) long that could go far out into the ocean or navigate narrow streams.

Archaeological research suggests that fishing was the prime activity of the early Mi'kmaq—nearly all excavated fire sites include burnt fish bones. Anecdotal records suggest that fishing before the arrival of Europeans was excellent, far beyond what it is today. The early French colonialist Nicolas Denys wrote in the seventeenth century, "If the pigeons bothered us by their large numbers, the salmon give us even more trouble."[3]

Beyond fishing, the communities participated in numerous activities such as painting and music and enjoyed a loose social order. Communities were formed by alliances and family relations. Leadership of the communities was based on prestige rather than physical or military might, and leaders were primarily concerned with successfully managing the fishing and hunting economy. Communities varied, however, in their patterns. While many remained essentially stationary around the bays and rivers, others hunted in the wooded uplands during the winter and came down to the seashores in the summer for shellfishing and leadership congresses. Mi'k-

maq communities encouraged speechmaking and storytelling as important cultural expressions, customs that persist in modern Mi'kmaq communities.

■ *Halifax-area Mi'kmaq, depicted here circa early 1800s, gradually adapted to centuries of contact with Europeans.*

The Decline of Native Culture

The arrival of Europeans in the 1500s brought profound changes for the Mi'kmaq and the Maliseet. Both First Nations welcomed the Europeans as trading partners, initially in the fish trade and then in the fur trade. They served as intermediaries, helping the Europeans expand their trade westward. In general, both the Mi'kmaq and the Maliseet closely aligned themselves with the French, an alliance that lasted when armed conflicts erupted between the French and British.

The Mi'kmaq and Maliseet thrived on the fur and fishing trade for about one hundred years, but European diseases decimated their communities, killing 75 percent or more of the people. In the case of the Maliseet, when the fur trade collapsed in the eighteenth century, Maliseet women shifted the

■ Glooskap and the Formation of Humans

In the language of the Mi'kmaq and other Algonquin tribes, *Glooskap* means "Man from Nothing"—the first person, according to Mi'kmaq tradition, to live on earth. In *How Glooskap Outwits the Ice Giants and Other Tales of the Maritime Indians*, writer and translator Howard Norman says that Glooskap "was a great hero and teacher. He taught people how they should live, about spiritual power, and how to overcome the obstacles that face mankind."

According to legend, Glooskap traveled extensively from Nova Scotia across the Bay of Fundy and down to New England. Along the way he did many great things. Having created animals that were as giant as he, Glooskap realized he was lonely and decided to create humans. But he feared how the giant animals would treat humans. When he asked the moose, bear, and squirrel individually, he learned they would mistreat humans. So Glooskap shrunk them and all other animals down to the size they are today and created humans. When humans first appeared, the other animals laughed at humans walking on two feet and told Glooskap that he had quite a sense of humor.

Maliseet economy to agriculture along the Saint John River. European settlers, however, eventually usurped Maliseet lands. In the nineteenth century, the Maliseet peoples began living on reserves (reservations) set aside by the government.

The Mi'kmaq suffered similarly. When the British eventually won control of the maritime area, they tried to force the Mi'kmaq into farming—a move that proved disastrous for a people accustomed to hunting and fur trading. Later, in the nineteenth and twentieth centuries, the Mi'kmaq made a transition to labor in crafts, lumber, and rail industries, but their consignment to reserves isolated them and left their society reeling.

The First European Explorers

The earliest history of exploration in the maritime provinces is a matter of debate. Historians think the Vikings who came to Newfoundland five hundred years before Christopher Columbus arrived in America may have made their way as far south as New Brunswick and explored the Gulf of St. Lawrence. If so, they left few traces—the archaeological site at

L'Anse aux Meadows in northern Newfoundland remains the only documented Viking site in North America. The first recorded exploration was by John Cabot in 1497, who made Nova Scotia part of his journeys and claimed it for Britain. Giovanni da Verrazano, an Italian explorer sailing for France, followed in 1524 and applied the name *Archadia* to a region along the Atlantic coast near Delaware. The name, according to his diaries, was a reference to the beauty of the trees in the area. Various explorers and map experts moved the name further up the coast, but by the 1620s, the term *Acadia* applied to the area of the maritime provinces, and it now refers particularly to the French-speaking areas of the provinces, especially that in New Brunswick and Nova Scotia.

Jacques Cartier came to the Gulf of St. Lawrence in 1534 and claimed all of the surrounding land for France. According to David Stanley, "Canada probably got its name from Cartier. *Kanata,* a Huron-Iroquois word for 'village' or 'small community,' showed up in Cartier's journal, and European mapmakers later transformed it into 'Canada.' The name was used for the St. Lawrence area and eventually became the official name of the new country."[4]

Almost no one followed Cartier into the area until just after the turn of the century. The first real attempt at settlement came in 1604 under the guidance of the French explorer and trader Pierre Du Gua de Monts. Along with fellow organizers Samuel de Champlain and Baron de Poutrincourt, de Monts and colony spent the winter on St. Croix Island, a tiny island on the present international border with Maine. The French originally chose the St. Croix spot because it provided a good place to anchor and easy defense against invaders. But the colony was ill-prepared for what followed. Winter was brutal, there was no fresh water or firewood on the island, and disease ran rampant. Of the eighty people who first came, thirty-six died of scurvy (now known to be from a lack of vitamin C). Survival for the rest depended on Mi'kmaq intervention that prevented starvation.

The next summer, the colonists dismantled their homes and rebuilt them at Port Royal on the north shore of the Annapolis Basin near the mouth of the Annapolis River. This new settlement proved a bit more prosperous. The people established a community around a central garden, the first European experimental seed plot in North America. In time, the colony established the first social club in North America and staged the first European theater event on the continent. But the hoped for prosperity did not materialize, and the settlers abandoned Port Royal in 1607. A former settler returned in 1610 and re-established the colony, but it was destroyed three years later by the British. The site changed hands numerous times over the years, with the British renaming it Annapolis Royal after taking it in 1710, but remained an important symbol of the European arrival.

■ *Explorer Pierre Du Gua de Monts was a leading figure in establishing France's earliest settlement in North America.*

■ Re-Creating Port Royal

In the early twentieth century the Canadian government began to appreciate what was lost when the original Port Royal settlement was abandoned and destroyed. After all, this was the site of France's first permanent settlement in North America and the earliest European settlement in North America north of Saint Augustine, Florida. In the late 1930s the Canadian government began to reconstruct the original Port Royal, as near to its original location as could be determined. The courtyard design was based on original sketches made by de Champlain and the buildings were constructed and furnished using seventeenth-century techniques and materials. The attention to detail and the costumed interpreters have helped to make Port Royal National Historic Site one of the most popular attractions in the maritimes and a fascinating glimpse into French colonial life in the early 1600s.

The Battle for Dominance

Armed conflict marred much of the exploration and settlement of the maritime provinces. Early on, rival French traders battled each other over territory along the Saint John River. This was soon replaced by conflict with the British. The area around the Saint John River stayed primarily in native hands for many years, but the French used it to launch raids against New England and the British well into the 1690s, creating a British hostility toward the French that lasts in some parts to the present day. Meanwhile, French settlers, who came to be known as Acadians, spread out from Port Royal and occupied much of present-day New Brunswick. The settlers used diking technology that allowed them to farm marshy areas created by the Bay of Fundy's tides. French fishermen plied the waters around Ile Saint-Jean, now known as Prince Edward Island.

The British battled with the French almost constantly after attacking Port Royal in 1613. In 1621, the British king James I granted Acadia (defined as all the land between New England and Newfoundland) to Sir William Alexander. A colonizer, Alexander never actually visited the area though he left his mark by renaming it New Scotland. Latin-loving British and Scots rendered this "Nova Scotia," a name that first began to appear on maps about a century later. Two Scottish settlements sprang up, then failed, but British colonization of present-day Nova Scotia and New Brunswick persisted, even as armed conflict among the French and English residents mounted.

After skirmishing for control of the maritimes throughout much of the seventeenth century, the British and French signed a treaty in 1713 that at least temporarily halted hostilities between the two countries. The Treaty of Utrecht mainly dealt with complex European issues but it also gave control of Acadia, the vaguely defined French corridor of present-day New Brunswick and Nova Scotia, to the British, while the French retained control of Ile Saint-Jean and Ile Royale (Cape Breton Island). Although the treaty was meant to resolve many long-term land issues, more conflict was to follow.

The Buildup to Conflict

Despite the Treaty of Utrecht, French settlement continued even in British-ruled areas—the Acadians in present-day Nova Scotia grew from two thousand in 1710 to twelve thousand in 1750. While British settlement would not begin in earnest until the 1740s, and few settled on Ile Saint-Jean (there were just seven hundred European settlers as late as 1748), the French also built up Louisbourg on Ile Royale. Louisbourg dominated the cod trade and became a major North American naval base for France.

In 1744 war broke out between the British and French. Fought on both sides of the Atlantic, it came to be known in Canada as King George's War. In 1745 British-backed forces attacked the heavily fortified Louisbourg and, after laying siege, caused it to surrender. In the meantime, the British attacked French shipping routes and ruined French trade in the maritimes. In 1748, a treaty ended the war and gave Louisbourg back to France. The treaty was so dissatisfying, however, that it set the stage for another major war within a few years.

Between the two wars, England more aggressively pursued settlement of its territory. In 1749, the British appointed Edward Cornwallis as governor of Nova Scotia and sent him with 2,500 settlers to establish a capital. The newcomers built the town of Chebucto, soon renamed Halifax, on an excellent natural harbor on the island's eastern shore. (Lt. General Charles Cornwallis, Edward's nephew, would later become famous for surrendering at the Battle of Yorktown in 1781, effectively ending the American Revolutionary War.)

These early settlers faced many difficulties, including occasional raids by Mi'kmaq bands, a short growing season

for crops, and cold winters. In spite of the troubles, other immigrants from England soon followed, strengthening the town's base and power. Many Germans also came to settle in Lunenburg and other south coast towns, notes writer Mary Duenwald:

■ *A drawing of the British built Halifax in the 1750s as a military and port town.*

> Unlike most Nova Scotians, whose ancestors were English, Irish and Scottish, Lunenburg residents largely trace their heritage to Germany. In the mid-1700s, the province's British government moved to counteract the threat posed by French settlers, the Acadians, who practiced Catholicism and resisted British rule. The provincial government enticed Protestants in southwestern Germany to immigrate to Nova Scotia by offering them tax-free land grants, surmising they would not sympathize with either the unruly Acadians or the American revolutionaries in the colonies to the south.[5]

When the French and Indian War opened in 1754, Nova Scotia was positioned to dominate the French throughout Acadia.

The Expulsion of the Acadians

The French and Indian War, which merged with the Seven Years' War when fighting broke out in Europe in 1756 and lasted through 1763, was a global confrontation between Britain and its allies on one side and France and its allies (including Russia and Spain) on the other. The war in North America began in the Ohio Valley when George Washington's troops ambushed a French military group. It quickly spread north to the maritime area of Canada, where the British laid plans to end the threat of Fort Beauséjour, a French military stronghold near present-day Sackville, New Brunswick. For two weeks in 1755, the British laid siege to the fort, before finally overrunning it.

The result was disastrous for the Acadians. After the Treaty of Utrecht, the British had insisted that all Acadians take an oath of loyalty to the British throne. The Acadians had refused, with some vowing allegiance to France and others saying they would stay neutral, and their settlements had spread, to the chagrin of the small British contingent. But the overthrow of Fort Beauséjour changed all that. The British insisted that all Acadians take the oath, and when they refused, the British ordered them to leave the territory.

Governor Charles Lawrence's plan to expel the Acadians was thought out long in advance and involved careful planning on the part of the military. During the summer of 1755, British soldiers seized guns from Acadians. The British per-

■ From Longfellow's "Evangeline: A Tale of Acadia"

This is the forest primeval; but where are the hearts that beneath it
Leaped like the roe, when he hears in the woodland the voice of
   the huntsman?
Where is the thatch-roofed village, the home of Acadian farmers—
Men whose lives glided on like rivers that water the woodlands,
Darkened by shadows of earth, but reflecting an image of heaven?
Waste are those pleasant farms, and the farmers forever departed!
Scattered like dust and leaves, when the mighty blasts of October
Seize them, and whirl them aloft, and sprinkle them far o'er the ocean.
Naught but tradition remains of the beautiful village of Grand-Pre.

Henry Wadsworth Longfellow, 1847

mitted the Acadians to continue to farm their lands through the summer so that they could bring in as much of their harvest as possible. Once the Acadians were gone, the British could then use the harvest.

In a typical instance, the Acadian men in a small agricultural area near Minas, Nova Scotia, were ordered to their local church. There, Lawrence read the governor's decree that the Acadians be expelled. Armed soldiers surrounded the stunned men and took them into custody. They were not allowed to leave the church, though small parties of men each day were permitted to go down to their families, and families were permitted to visit the men until they had prepared sufficiently to leave.

■ Ships wait to deport hundreds of Acadians from Grand Pré, near Windsor on the Bay of Fundy, in the 1760s.

A Heartbreaking Ending

The experience was different from place to place, and the Acadians at Chignecto even resisted successfully for a time, killing a British major and twenty-four of his men. In the end, though, they all wound up on boats and wagons headed out of British-dominated Nova Scotia. The result was heartbreaking for the Acadians and today is still a source of tension between French and English descendants. Ten thousand Acadians were forced from their homes and lands. They were allowed to leave with their families and whatever they could reasonably put in their wagons. General John Winslow, who oversaw the expulsion, in guilt recorded, "It hurts me to hear their weeping & waling and nashing of teeth, I am in hopes our affairs will soon put on another face and we get transports and I [am] rid of the worst peace of service ever I was in."[6]

Many Acadians found temporary refuge on Ile Saint-Jean, which the British called Isle St. John. (It was not renamed Prince Edward Island until 1799.) The population there ballooned to forty-five hundred, but dropped when the British once again seized Fort Louisbourg in 1758. Expelled from the island, some Acadians tried to return home (only to be expelled again), others headed back to France, and many went to the American colonies. Although Britain prevailed over France in the Seven Years' War, the 1763 Treaty of Paris permitted the Acadians to return. When they did, however, many found their lands occupied by British settlers. Approximately two thousand Acadians resettled in Nova Scotia, particularly around Clare, while many others settled along the Saint John River in today's New Brunswick.

Immigrants Shape the Provinces

The Treaty of Paris effectively ended open hostilities and began a period of aggressive but peaceful settlement in the maritimes. Over the next few decades the provinces were reshaped to today's borders. Prince Edward Island and Cape Breton were made part of Nova Scotia just after the war, but only temporarily. Prince Edward Island became a separate colony in 1769, and Cape Breton Island separated from Nova Scotia 1784, only to rejoin in 1820.

Meanwhile, the British worked to populate their newly won territory, and settlers from Europe and the United States found the maritimes hospitable. To promote settlement of Prince Edward Island, writer Will Ferguson comments, "The island was surveyed into lots, and the lots were drawn in a lottery and awarded to patrons back in Britain who were required to ship in tenant farmers to break the land."[7] This had a major long-term effect, Ferguson notes, since the island never renounced its colonial status and thus could eventually become a province, unlike the larger island of Cape Breton. Ferguson writes:

> The roots of [Prince Edward] Island autonomy date back to 1769, when it was separated from Nova Scotia and made into a distinct colony complete with its own governor and an elaborate constitution. One of the reasons Britain granted P.E.I. special status lay in the unique manner in which it was settled. Alone among the colonies of British North America, P.E.I. was owned entirely by absentee land-lords. It was an experiment, a pet project of British dandies looking to build their own little Edens in the New World.[8]

The land division caused settlement on Prince Edward Island to begin in earnest. The American Revolution brought an influx of "United Empire Loyalists," settlers who favored the British during the revolution and who fled (or were expelled by) the conquering Americans, but the largest growth came from Great Britain between 1798 and 1850 when the population went from four thousand to sixty-two thousand.

In Nova Scotia, early growth came from both Europe and America. New Englanders were mainly responsible for pushing

■ *United Empire Loyalists, like those arriving here at the site of Saint John in 1783, helped to establish New Brunswick.*

Halifax's population from eight thousand in 1763 to seventeen thousand in 1775. In 1784, Loyalists from the newly independent American colonies flooded north after the defeat of the British army. Roughly thirty thousand Loyalists came to Nova Scotia during this time, more than doubling the existing population. Fourteen thousand settled on the western shore of the Bay of Fundy, established the city of Saint John, and began infiltrating the Saint John River valley. The others were dispersed throughout Nova Scotia and Cape Breton. The strain from the immigrants was so great and the identities of the separate people so distinct that those on the west side of the Bay of Fundy petitioned Great Britain for the right to form a separate government. In 1784 Nova Scotia was officially separated, with the new colony being named New Brunswick in honor of the House of Brunswick, the ancestors of Britain's king George III. The Cape Breton split was also caused by the arrival of the Loyalists.

Building the Provincial Economies

As immigrants came, the provinces formed their economic identities. Prince Edward Island's chief asset was rich farmland that drew thousands of British settlers. The British parceling of

■ *In early–nineteenth century winters, New Brunswick woodsmen used oxen-pulled sleds to haul logs for shipbuilding through the woods to the riverbank.*

land created a furor between tenants who paid unfair rents and landowners, many of whom were uninterested in their land or in settlement. Even so, the promise of land brought thousands to the small island, and Prince Edward Island became a major producer of potatoes and other crops.

New Brunswick grew almost entirely on the strength of a thriving timber industry. The Napoleonic Wars in Europe during the early 1800s and the War of 1812 in America and then the American Civil War from 1861 to 1865 fueled the hunger for timber to build ships. New Brunswick loggers and shipbuilders combined to churn out more than one hundred ships per year. Over time, however, the reliance on shipbuilding and fishing was also a curse to the province, since economic events elsewhere in the world could cause major downturns in the local economy.

Nova Scotia followed a similar pattern, growing from timber and fishing and becoming world-renowned for its outstanding wooden sailing ships. Like New Brunswick, Nova Scotia benefited when distant wars supported its shipbuilding industry. Nova Scotia was a key launching place for privateers—government-hired pirates who seized enemy ships and took home loads of profit.

Toward Confederation

When the timber and shipbuilding industries began to falter after the end of the American Civil War, and trade restrictions caused exports to taper off, the maritime colonies' economies suffered. Because the colonies shared sea resources and similar economies, some residents called for their unification under one government. During the early 1860s leaders from Canada West (Ontario) and Canada East (Quebec) were also taking the first steps toward forming a confederation that would be independent of Great Britain. They considered crucial the participation of New Brunswick, Nova Scotia, Prince Edward Island, and Newfoundland. The historic convention that set the stage for the formation of Canada was held in Charlottetown in 1864, which is why Prince Edward Island's capital is sometimes called "the birthplace of Canada."

The nation-building process succeeded three years later when Great Britain passed the British North America Act, establishing Canada as a separate entity. New Brunswick and Nova Scotia joined Quebec and Ontario as the first four

provinces of the new nation. Prince Edward Island, more separate in identity from its sister provinces, resisted confederation until 1873, when a severe debt incurred by a costly railroad building project caused them to seek relief from the Canadian government. Newfoundland did not become a province until 1949.

Ultimately, confederation did little to ease the challenges facing the three provinces. The lack of economic diversity hurt all three provinces during and after confederation, and the new federal government took steps that further weakened the provinces. Confederation was only a step in a long series of challenges to follow.

Strength Through Diversity

Confederation was an enormous change for the maritime provinces but it represented at best a mixed blessing. While Nova Scotia, New Brunswick, and Prince Edward Island were now connected to a government on the mainland, they suffered economically in the years to follow. In part, the maritime provinces were to blame for the hard times. They had not diversified their economies and were thus subject to sharp downturns when the products they made fell out of favor. But federal policy relating to the maritimes also proved disastrous. In particular, a series of protective tariffs—taxes on imports and exports—crippled maritime trade with the United States.

By the time World War II ended, the maritime provinces were far behind the rest of Canada in quality of life and social services. Only within recent years have a series of government programs, both federal and provincial, begun to offer a renewed sense of hope for the maritime provinces.

A Center for Trading

The years immediately before and after confederation were crucial ones for the maritime provinces. Since the 1840s, when a treaty with the United States had lowered the taxes placed on traded goods, the maritimes had enjoyed a vigorous commerce with it and other countries. Halifax thrived as a center for banking and trade, with the port busily shipping goods to Europe and New England. Entrepreneurs built steel mills, cotton mills, sugar refineries, and other manufacturing

■ *Nova Scotia farmers hold a plowing contest shortly after confederation.*

plants in the maritimes. Huge sailing ships delivered finished goods to European and American ports.

Nova Scotia's Annapolis Valley and other parts of the maritimes even produced and exported agricultural commodities. According to a historical overview of Nova Scotia's Western Valley Development Authority,

> Due to the large number of merchant ships owned by Nova Scotians during the Golden Age of Sail, the produce from this area was transported to markets near and far. Shiploads of apples sailed to the British Isles. Livestock, field crops and fruit were dispatched to the New England States (referred to as the Boston States) and to the other British Colonies. A significant amount of produce also was shipped to the Caribbean islands.[9]

By the late 1870s Saint John shipbuilders were launching two ships per week. This made Saint John the fourth largest shipbuilding city in the world and earned it the nickname "the Liverpool of America" (after Great Britain's leading shipbuilding city of the era). Saint John began to rival Halifax as a hub for communication and trade.

Harmful Tax Policies

The maritime provinces' heyday as a trading center proved to be temporary. The post–Civil War period saw both the United States and Canada adopt more restrictive trading policies. Canada decided it needed to become more independent of the United States and to develop its own industrial base. Both countries began to use taxes on traded goods to control imports and exports. In Canada, import duties on raw materials were lowered in order to keep production costs low. This policy had the effect of encouraging industrial growth in Ontario and Quebec. For the maritimes, however, it meant that trading with the United States became more costly.

The maritime provinces' complaint to Ottawa that demand for maritime-produced materials was being unfairly stifled fell on deaf ears. The maritimes managed to weather some of the initial difficulties. For a time it appeared that they might be able to sustain themselves on trade with central Canada and Great Britain. "That was short-lived," notes maritime economist Fred McMahon. He explains:

> Industry may have been located in the Maritimes, but the population base was a thousand miles away in Central Canada. That made no sense in an age when goods were heavier than today and transportation costs considerably higher. Central Canadian interests began to buy out Maritime businesses. The businesses weren't immediately shut down, but investment was stifled. New plants were built where the market was concentrated—Central Canada.[10]

The resulting economic fallout caused thousands of residents to leave New Brunswick and Nova Scotia and head south to the United States.

A Bitter Pill

For Nova Scotia, the matter of confederation was a particularly bitter pill. The provinces were not yet connected to the rest of Canada by rail, though Nova Scotia had begun operating railroads on its land in the 1850s. Residents of Nova Scotia believed that their maritime-based economy would suffer greatly (as it did) without connection to the larger Canadian economy. Further, they resented the change in orientation— many Nova Scotians considered themselves more closely aligned with Great Britain than with the rest of Canada, and

■ Black Wednesday:
The Fire that Destroyed Saint John

On touring Saint John in the 1860s, according to the website for New Brunswick Community College Saint John, a *Boston Gazette* writer described the architecture as being "dignified without pretence and substantial without pride or show." Unfortunately, many of these impressive buildings were made of wood.

The winds blew hard on June 2, 1877, but otherwise it was a nice, late-spring day in Saint John when fire broke out at York Point, today's Market Square. The winds rapidly fanned the fire, and before long, hundreds of buildings and homes were in flames. Nine hours later, when firefighters finally extinguished the blaze, eighteen people were dead, thirteen thousand were left homeless, and the residential and business center of the city was destroyed. The fire caused more than $28 million in damage, only 25 percent of which was insured, and left the city reeling.

But Saint John's devastation was the world's opportunity to help. Communities throughout the maritimes, North America, and Great Britain sent donations, supplies, and workers such as architects, masons, and engineers to help rebuild the city. In just five years, the city was completely rebuilt—this time with brick and other materials that would slow the spread of fire and reduce the loss of life.

■ *Saint John's Custom House was one of the many notable buildings ravaged by the Great Fire of 1877.*

they believed their economy was better supported by shipping between Great Britain.

While Nova Scotia joined the confederation in 1867, it did so only after a popular anticonfederation campaign failed to sway the legislative assembly. (The confederation decision was not decided by popular election.) In 1869 Governor Joseph Howe, a political icon in Nova Scotia who had led the anticonfederation movement, negotiated with the federal government for "better terms" for Nova Scotia. In exchange for promised federal subsidies Nova Scotia agreed to become a full and active participant in the new confederation. Even so, resentment lingered. Calls for secession multiplied as Nova Scotia's economy gradually declined in the late nineteenth century.

Like its sister provinces, Prince Edward Island suffered from the restrictive trade policy and saw its industry and population begin to drop. Even though Prince Edward Island had been the host of the 1864 conference that had launched the drive to confederation, it had quickly distanced itself from

■ *Joseph Howe was a powerful champion of self-government in his native Nova Scotia.*

■ Nova Scotia's Bum Deal

July 1, 1867, was a hated day almost immediately for many Nova Scotians. They felt that the rest of Canada was looking to strip Nova Scotia of its identity and take away its ability to survive economically so that the rest of the confederation could have its separate government and strong interior manufacturing. On Confederation Day, the *Eastern Chronicle and Pictou County Advocate* carried mock marriage, birth, and death notices that called Nova Scotia a young bride forced into an unhappy marriage, the Confederation an "infant monster," and the prosperous life of Nova Scotians dead at the hands of "Dr. Poison Bag."

That fall, Nova Scotians sent to parliament thirty-six anticonfederate representatives out of thirty-eight available seats. Governor Howe's 1869 agreement with the federal government calling for greater government subsidies only temporarily eased Nova Scotians' bitterness. By 1886, these were forgotten as Nova Scotia elected to parliament twenty-six representatives who favored repeal. While the political climate for repeal gradually faded, simmering public anger did not. As late as the 1920s, many people of Nova Scotia still flew the flag at half-mast on Confederation Day.

such talk. The debt incurred with its railroad building caused the province to seek federal help and join the union in 1873. Of course, the railroad did not connect to the mainland, so the potential for industry was limited. While agriculture remained steady, it was hampered by the expense of shipping off the island. The population of Prince Edward Island reached a nineteenth-century high of 109,000 in 1891, but the draw of western work was too much. An erosion in population began that would leave only 88,000 on the island by the arrival of the Great Depression in the early 1930s.

Railroads to the Rescue

The maritime provinces recognized many of the challenges they faced and sought to stave off some of the coming economic problems. One of the appeals of confederation had related to promises that the federal government would help fund the building of railroads that would connect the maritimes with markets in central Canada. The Intercolonial Railway had been in negotiation since 1862, and an 1864 deal had guaranteed that work would start after confederation. Sure enough, in 1867, shortly after New Brunswick and Nova Scotia entered the confederation, construction began.

The construction project brought jobs to the provinces, since engineers, builders, and laborers were needed. Further, the railroad connected New Brunswick and Nova Scotia to each other and to the rest of Canada as they never had been before. The first lines in the provinces opened in 1872, and the project was essentially finished in 1876. While the Intercolonial Railway was never a huge financial success, it caused towns to spring up in its path, and it increased trade with the rest of Canada. The federal government used subsidies to keep the cost of shipping freight low. The Intercolonial Railway was providing regular passenger train service to Montreal by the turn of the century.

In its early years the new railroad helped promote further industrialization in the provinces. As shipbuilding and

■ *Intercolonial Railway workers use massive stones to construct a culvert near Nova Scotia's Black River in 1871.*

forestry started to decline, and the manufacturing industries such as textiles, iron, and sugar were hurt by trade policies, central Canadian firms began buying up maritime businesses. Because these businesses were remote from much of mainland Canada, many of them failed to modernize sufficiently and were eventually closed. In the end, the downward trend continued until World War I.

War and Depression

The First World War was a temporary economic salve for the three provinces, though it cost them in lives. Further, the war brought social changes to the maritimes. Saint John became a key shipping point for weapons, food, horses, machinery, and troops headed overseas. Halifax was a critical naval base and a launching point for ships carrying troops and munitions. Halifax ships lived in constant fear of attack, and the city was on guard throughout the war for signs of naval strikes or even invasion. The city's worst war injuries, however, were self-inflicted. In 1917 two ships in the harbor collided, triggering an explosion that was the largest human-made blast before the nuclear age. Prince Edward Island, though not a key port for shipping, sent soldiers and supplies in World War I and saw many of its men killed and wounded.

The increased shipping boosted the area's economy, but the war drew many of the men into battle overseas. For the first time, significant numbers of women entered the workforce. Women worked as nurses and clerks in the armed forces, and they held positions in business, industry, and agriculture. Although women workers were generally supplanted by men after the war, the war was a factor in winning women the right to vote in Canada. Women in the armed services won the right to vote in federal elections in 1917, and all women in 1918. Over the next few years all three maritime provinces granted women the right to vote in provincial elections.

The end of World War I decreased shipping demand and hurt the economies of the provinces again. The gradual slide of unemployment and deteriorating social services continued through the 1920s and were exacerbated by the Great Depression. Though World War II revived many of the industries dormant since World War I, federal policies continued to favor central Canadian manufacturing industries. By the 1940s, the

The Great Halifax Explosion

On December 6, 1917, the Belgian ship *Imo* and the French ship *Mont Blanc*, which carried more than 400,000 pounds of TNT among other explosives, were maneuvering in the Halifax harbor area. A miscommunication put them in each other's path, and additional mistakes caused a collision. The collision started a fire on the *Mont Blanc* that raged for twenty minutes. As the fire spread, the ship brushed a pier and set it on fire. Fire crews responded quickly and began to fight the blaze. Meanwhile, people in the area gathered to see the blaze and watch the firefighters at work. Suddenly, the *Mont Blanc* blew up in a mammoth explosion.

The blast immediately killed more than 1,900 people, with the death toll rising above 2,000 within a year. An additional 9,000 people were injured. Glass that shattered in people's faces as they watched the fire through windows was responsible for about 1,000 of the injuries. Nearly all of the north end of Halifax was destroyed, and fires burned down many surrounding buildings.

The blast was so powerful that it hurled *Mont Blanc's* half-ton anchor shank more than two miles (three kilometers) from the site. Residents of Sydney, Cape Breton, 270 miles (435 kilometers) away, felt the shock wave. Hospitals were overwhelmed, and conditions in the city worsened the next day when a blizzard dumped more than a foot of snow on the wreckage and made recovery more difficult. Rebuilding efforts began immediately, and Halifax recovered, but the incident has forever haunted the city.

■ *Canadian soldiers were among the many rescue workers that helped Halifax recover after the massive harbor explosion of 1917.*

standard of living in the maritime provinces was well below that of the rest of Canada.

Social Problems Beset the Provinces

The economic struggles of the maritime provinces led to an assortment of challenging social problems. For instance, by the 1940s, New Brunswick spent barely more than half the national average on education and health care services. Its illiteracy and infant mortality rates ranked at the top of the country. Worse, there were disparities within the province that created animosity and tension. Rural French areas in the north had far less access to basic services and a far lower standard of living than did the English-dominated southern cities.

Nova Scotia fared somewhat better economically during World War II, but suffered similar social problems. Toward the end of the war, Halifax was overcrowded and unruly because of the swell of troops. Lawlessness occasionally reigned, with riots occurring on the day the war ended in Europe. Problems continued after the war. Construction on the Saint Lawrence Seaway began, which meant that icebreakers would soon be able to reach interior North America in the dead of winter, thus further weakening Nova Scotia's role as an eastern shipping port. Halifax's role as a military asset dwindled and military personnel were moved to other sites.

Surrounding areas also faced similar challenges. The 1955 completion of the imposing Angus L. Macdonald Bridge, which joined Dartmouth and Halifax, revitalized Dartmouth by allowing large cargo ships to pass underneath. In a population boom more than twenty thousand people moved to the area. But basic services were hard to sustain—the new residents dealt with unpaved roads and too few schools.

Prince Edward Island's isolation gave it a sense of proud independence but also hindered the development of basic services. Until the 1950s, the island had only one ferry that made just a few trips per day between the island and the mainland. Thus, the tourist economy was essentially dead, and shipping was slow. The island did not even permit car travel on roads until 1919, and though that changed, few roads were actually developed until the 1950s. Further, as writer Ian Darragh explains, "On P.E.I. change has often come slowly. Some parts of the island got paved roads and 'the lights,' as electricity was called, only in the early sixties. The 1970s finally saw the demise of the one-room schoolhouse."[11]

The Maritimes Modernize

As early as 1940 a government report had revealed many of the startling inequalities developing between the maritime provinces and the rest of Canada. Recommended changes were slow to come, however, with the federal government not acting earnestly to improve conditions in the maritimes until the early 1960s.

In New Brunswick, the champion for reform and "equal opportunity" was Louis J. Robichaud, the first elected Acadian premier of New Brunswick. With increased federal funding at his disposal, Robichaud pushed through legislation that changed how New Brunswick operated. The province took control of services like education, welfare, health care, and administration of justice, and it left to towns services like fire control and police protection. Robichaud also pursued a policy of aggressive industrialization. His government poured money into mining, electricity generation, and forestry, and the province put in major highways in the north to facilitate transportation and shipping. Federal money subsidized the shipment of goods to the rest of Canada and brought New Brunswick into active

■ Louis J. Robichaud: The First Acadian Premier

Louis J. Robichaud knew from an early age what he would be later in his life: In a graduating class time capsule, he signed his name "Louis J. Robichaud, Premier of New Brunswick." Robichaud became leader of the Liberal party in October 1958, then won the premier's seat in 1960. He won reelection in 1963 and 1967, then lost his seat in the 1970 election.

Robichaud is often called the most influential premier in the province's history. His "Equal Opportunity" program vaulted the province into the modern era, although political opponents saw it as an enormous government power grab and a threat to New Brunswick's traditional way of life. Robichaud was particularly important to Acadians. His election elevated Acadians to equal status with their fellow citizens. Further, Robichaud's government established and funded the Université de Moncton to enhance Acadian education and culture. It made French an official language by passing the "Official Languages Act" of 1969, thus guaranteeing Acadians access to government and social services in their native language. Though controversial, Robichaud's policies and beliefs continue to influence much of New Brunswick public service today.

■ *Cape Breton coal miners, shown here pausing for a lunch break in 1946, have seen their jobs dwindle in recent years.*

competition with other provinces' industries. The results were largely successful. Today the province enjoys far better schooling, transportation, and health care and ranks competitively with the rest of Canada in many social areas.

From the 1950s on, Nova Scotia's chief concern was establishing sufficient industries to boost its economy and keep vital services going. In 1955 Nova Scotia began construction on an international airport. The province latched onto the British idea of industrial parks—Volvo and other major companies established plants in Nova Scotia because of Industrial Estates Limited, the government-organized group that encouraged industrial development. Increased federal funds enabled the provincial government to become more actively involved in the economy in other ways, as well. When the struggling coal industry seemed on the verge of collapse, the government formed the Cape Breton Development Corporation and encouraged innovative new fuel solutions. (The company today mixes coal, water, and chemicals to make a unique fuel.) The government has been involved in other industries as well and in general has succeeded in raising the standard of living and becoming more competitive with New Brunswick and the rest of Canada.

Change on Prince Edward

On Prince Edward Island, change has come more gradually. The economy remained centered on fishing and agriculture even as federal funds helped to build new roads and schools

■ The Marvelous—and Controversial— Confederation Bridge

For residents of Prince Edward Island, the completion of Confederation Bridge in June 1997 was either long overdue or represents a detestable new threat to the island's unique character. It seems that there are few moderate opinions.

The massive bridge spanning the Northumberland Strait to New Brunswick is the world's longest bridge over ice-covered saltwater. Able to carry as many as four thousand vehicles per hour, the bridge put an end to the two- and three-hour waits summer travelers faced to take a forty-five-minute ferry ride to the island. It has thus contributed to easier transport of goods as well as to a large jump in tourism.

But not all island residents and businesses welcomed it. Fishermen believed that the bridge would interfere with the migratory patterns of lobsters and fish, threatening the fishing industry. Others feared that the island would be overrun with ever-increasing numbers of visitors and would lose its rural charm. The tension between residents was palpable. The island tradition of keeping peace by avoiding confrontations over issues went by the wayside. The subject of the bridge could not be avoided, and the debate was often rancorous.

Now that it has been operating for a number of years, the effect of the bridge remains controversial. The fishing appears not to have suffered greatly, although those in the industry say that it may still be too early to discern long-term patterns. On the other hand, the influx of visitors has been, if anything, even greater than expected.

■ *Graceful Confederation Bridge is the backdrop for a scenic Prince Edward Island sunset.*

on the island. Further, farming itself changed. In the first half of the century, most farms were family-owned and produced a variety of goods. Over the years, agribusiness has gradually increased, such that most mixed-product farms were located on the central north shore in the late 1990s. Potatoes have always been a major cash crop, but as Darragh says, the emphasis changed: "Small family farms have given way to agribusinesses—operations of up to 3,000 acres that grow potatoes to feed the North American appetite for french fries."[12]

Tourism has grown, as well, for the small province. A national park was established in the 1930s, but the province did little to develop it and little to attract tourists until the 1950s and 1960s. By the late 1990s, with the completion of Confederation Bridge, tourism had boomed into a massive industry, with more than 1 million visitors coming annually.

Looking to Diversify

While New Brunswick and Nova Scotia continued to promote fishing, mining, and forestry, they also branched into other industries. Nova Scotia established in 1987 that gas fields off of Sable Island would likely be profitable, so development and drilling began. Two other natural gas fields were discovered in 1992, and production started on those soon after. In addition, oil and gas exploration continued along the coasts of the province. New Brunswick diversified its mining efforts when gold was discovered in the center of the province. Further, the province started building a strong telecommunications sector that could help provide stability in the twenty-first century. Prince Edward Island found oil and natural gas off of its coasts, but in supplies too small for mining. While agriculture remained the main island focus, tourism and forestry increased.

The challenge for all three maritime provinces is now to secure the recent economic gains without sacrificing the region's unique identity. With the changes of the last forty years, the provinces are in a better position to compete with Canada's other provinces. Maritime residents love the scenery, the outdoor activities, and the industries that keep them close to land and sea. Not all of the social ills have been fixed, but the maritime provinces have improved greatly as a place to live.

Daily Life

I t might be tempting to think of today's maritime provinces as a somewhat sleepy area of fishing villages and small farms. Certainly, the provinces have their share of bucolic towns where people's lives are not all that changed from previous generations. On Prince Edward Island, even though the small land area means that the population density is greater than anywhere else in Canada, agriculture reigns and small-town living is the norm.

But the last several decades have also seen the maritimes embrace the same fast-paced, urban lifestyle that is the norm throughout much of North America. Each province has its own hubs of manufacturing, commerce, and high-tech industry, and in many ways, these urban centers have rejuvenated the maritimes. The maritimes enjoy a lively mix of nationalities and races, and cities provide the jobs created by the growing economies. Modern communications technology has made its way into communities and classrooms, connecting residents like never before and making them part of a larger global community.

Saint John's Melting Pot

Located on the Saint John River where it empties into the Bay of Fundy, Saint John is New Brunswick's largest city. It typifies the mix of people and lifestyles in the maritimes, and it illustrates the importance of larger cities to the region. Saint John is home to approximately seventy thousand residents, but during the day the population soars due to an influx of tens of thousands of commuters. Further, the surrounding suburbs bring the total population of the greater metropolitan area to more than 122,000 people, or about 20 percent of the entire provincial population.

■ Black Heritage in Saint John

Saint John was a key migration center for blacks in the eighteenth and nineteenth centuries, particularly during two eras. Some 3,000 free blacks who had fought with the British in the American Revolution and more than 1,000 slaves to Loyalist owners came to parts of present-day Nova Scotia and New Brunswick in 1783. All were promised land lots, but the distribution of these lots was muddled, and the few who received any land got so little that they could not farm for survival. In 1792, nearly 2,000 blacks left for Sierra Leone in Africa. But more Loyalist black immigrants arrived in the years after the War of 1812. Approximately 2,000 came, with about 500 settling in New Brunswick, principally in the Loch Lomond area.

Various schools were started over time in Loch Lomond, Elm Hill, and Willow Grove, and by the time slavery was abolished in 1834 in the British empire, there were no slaves in the maritimes. Much of today's African Canadian population descends from these early black immigrants.

■ *Blacks like the Shelburne, Nova Scotia, woodcutter depicted here in 1788 were among the many Loyalists who established communities in the maritimes after the American Revolution.*

Saint John enjoys a rich and diverse heritage. More than 90 percent of residents speak English at home, while roughly 5 percent speak either French alone or French and English equally. A small percentage speak German, Mi'kmaq, or some other tongue. The overwhelming majority of residents are of European heritage, and because of the Loyalist settlement after the American Revolution, most have English, Scottish, or Irish backgrounds. Although the black community in Saint John numbers only about one thousand, it is well established and has contributed prominent business people, politicians, and athletes to the city.

Saint John's close proximity to the sea makes it a shipping and fishing port, but the city is home to other industries as well. The city's unemployment rate in recent years has hovered around 8 percent, slightly lower than the provincial average. Only a small fraction of the city's workforce is employed in agriculture or in the energy industries of coal, oil, and natural gas. Roughly one in five persons works in the manufacturing and construction industries, which are expected to grow over the next several years. Saint John's recent prosperity has led to an increase in home building and new business ventures. For example, in 2002 the city announced it was establishing a new sugar refinery that would receive raw sugar by ship from Brazil and refine it for the Canadian market.

Much of the remainder of Saint John's workforce is employed in service-based industries such as retail sales, telecommunications services, government, and health care. The city's four hospitals and numerous health centers are major employers, and the city has seen recent growth in high-tech industries.

As with other places in the maritime provinces, social services have improved greatly in Saint John over the last forty years. The city has a strong transportation system with public

■ *The block-long Old City Market is a major retail site in Saint John.*

buses and a nearby airport. It is also home to the University of New Brunswick at Saint John and New Brunswick Community College, institutions that offer degrees and technical training to more than thirteen thousand students per year. Further, economic development has been a focus in the past decade. Organizations such as the Human Development Council provide services to upstart businesses and offer loans to low-income people that enable them to expand their businesses or buy necessities until they can get back to work.

Halifax: The Heart of Nova Scotia

With almost 360,000 people, Halifax is the heart of Nova Scotia, accounting for more than one-third of the province's total population. It is the largest city in the maritimes and the most diverse economically, racially, and socially. Its size and location—Halifax marks the halfway point between Europe and the west coast of Canada—makes it a hub for shipping, manufacturing, and trading throughout the maritime region.

Like Saint John, Halifax is made up predominantly of European descendants, particularly those who descended from Loyalist immigrants. But Halifax has a somewhat more diverse population, with blacks the largest minority at more than twelve thousand people. Many of Halifax's black citizens are descended from immigrants who came either after the American Revolution or after the War of 1812.

Halifax residents are employed in many of the same industries that Saint John's residents are. More than 85 percent hold service-based jobs, with about 10 percent in manufacturing and construction. The tiny contribution of the resource industries may increase in the near future—surveyors are measuring to see if natural gas discovered just outside of Halifax will be profitable to mine. The city and surrounding municipal area contain twelve business parks. Halifax is also home to oil and gas development companies, light industrial and warehousing businesses, and the largest concentration of retail companies in the maritime region.

The port at Halifax is particularly busy. According to Mark Morris, author of *Atlantic Canada Handbook*, to its residents "Halifax is more than a city, more than a seaport, and more than a provincial capital. Halifax is a harbor with a city attached."[13] In a typical year, Halifax receives and ships 10 million metric tons of cargo. Dockside facilities allow goods to be quickly transferred from ships to waiting cargo trains headed for Montreal,

Toronto, and the United States. Halifax's port generates $670 million in employment income each year and accounts for nine thousand direct and indirect jobs. But the port is hardly the only, or even key, employment opportunity in Halifax.

As with Saint John, Halifax is a bustling city situated conveniently near the sea where many fishermen still earn their livelihood. Halifax is home to twelve major hospitals and numerous community health centers. There are more than 170 parks for public enjoyment. The nearby airport receives 3 million passengers per year and ranks as the seventh busiest in Canada. The city offers higher education at seven universities and community colleges, including St. Mary's University and Nova Scotia Community College.

Charlottetown Thrives Amidst Farms

Of the one hundred forty thousand people living on Prince Edward Island, nearly sixty thousand live in the province's capital, Charlottetown. Charlottetown is situated on the south shore of central Prince Edward Island and is bordered by rivers on the east and west. Small by comparison to Saint John or Halifax, Charlottetown nevertheless has the feel of an

■ Principal Port in the Maritimes

What makes the port at Halifax so special? Halifax has one of the largest natural harbors in the world. It is deep enough to allow even huge ocean-going ships to dock. Moreover, the influence of offshore ocean currents keeps the port ice-free year-round.

While the port's main business is heavy cargo, it has become more involved in strengthening tourism and supporting the surrounding community. Halifax is a premier Atlantic cruise ship launching point, sending out more than ninety ships per year carrying some 150,000 passengers. The sea cruise business has grown so successfully in recent years that the port is investing millions of dollars to make needed improvements. Better traffic flow and new landscaping and building design have made the port area more pleasing for tourists and residents alike. The project could be the blueprint for a downtown revitalization project the port hopes to initiate.

The cruise industry is vital to the local economy. In 2001, visitors who came ashore from the cruise ships spent an average of almost $100 per person, totaling some $15 million. Thus, the port area has seen a steady growth of restaurants, shops, and other tourist attractions.

■ *Railway container terminals allow for efficient transport of goods from ships using the harbor at Halifax.*

urban center in the middle of a farm-dominated island. "There's a lot less stress living here," says Wayne Goodwin, a thirty-two-year-old researcher at Diagnostic Chemicals. "I have a house I could never afford in Toronto or Vancouver," he told *Maclean's* magazine. "I can go home for lunch or go out for a walk at night without hearing traffic and sirens."[14]

Charlottetown is the province's cultural, financial, and governmental center. A much higher percentage of the residents work in retail and tourism than in manufacturing or construction. Government service and health care also combine to make up substantial employment blocks—the two generate roughly one-quarter of the city's jobs.

Charlottetown is also the major transportation hub for the province. The city can be reached by just about all provincial residents within an hour. The Trans Canada Highway heads west from Charlottetown to the Confederation Bridge and on to the mainland. The Charlottetown Airport offers regional service, with daily flights to and from Halifax and Toronto. The bus and railway systems connect people within the city and link to the wider rail service available throughout the province. The city also has a small port that provides storage space, icebreaker support, and sewage disposal.

Finally, Charlottetown is Prince Edward Island's home for higher education. The University of Prince Edward Island offers programs in art, science, business administration, nursing, and veterinary medicine. Holland College, Prince Edward Island's community college, provides training and degrees in technology, business, tourism, communications, and other fields. More than three thousand full- and part-time students attend each school.

Ethnic Diversity in the Maritimes

Beyond the major metropolitan areas, the maritimes are a mix of cultures and races. The region was an important home for blacks migrating from the United States and Jamaica; many natives descend from the Mi'kmaq; and English, Scottish, French, and Irish peoples are well-represented. New Brunswick is

■ The Close-Knit People of Prince Edward Island

To residents of Prince Edward Island, one is truly an islander only by being born on the island. Someone who comes from anywhere else, at any point in his or her life, is "from away." While that may make Prince Edward Island sound close-knit and standoffish, the province is actually a welcoming place to newcomers as well as to the multitudes of tourists who come each year. Towns have a strong sense of community and family bonds endure.

As David Weale, a professor at the University of Prince Edward Island, told *National Geographic* magazine, true island residents are distinct in their personalities and entrenched in their lives: "We islanders still know who we are and where we belong. Like the woman who was asked if she had traveled much. 'No,' she said thoughtfully. 'Didn't have to. I was born here!'"

unique among Canada's provinces in that, with French and English as languages, it is officially bilingual.

Outside of Saint John, New Brunswick has an almost equal mix of French and English. Approximately 300,000 of New Brunswick's residents claim mixed ancestry. Of the more than 440,000 who claim a single ancestry, 28 percent name England, Scotland, or Ireland, and 26 percent France, with many other groups making up the remainder. French heritage is particularly strong in Moncton, the province's second largest city at 118,000, where more than 30 percent of the residents speak French. French speakers also predominate in the rural areas bordering Quebec's Gaspé Peninsula, such as Campbellton, where more than 50 percent of the residents speak French. The French influence has helped elect many prominent French-speaking politicians in New Brunswick, including Jean Chretien, Canada's prime minister since 1993, whom New Brunswick voters chose as a member of parliament in 1990.

Neither Nova Scotia nor Prince Edward Island has as many French-speaking residents as New Brunswick. Nova Scotia has the maritimes' highest concentration of First Nations people, numbering more than twelve thousand. Prince Edward Island's population is the least diverse of the three provinces, having very few blacks and only about a thousand natives.

■ *Canadian prime minister Jean Chretien and his wife Aline chat with shoppers at a Moncton mall while campaigning in New Brunswick during the fall of 2000.*

■ French Heritage in New Brunswick

The influence of French culture on New Brunswick is profound. French is an official language of the province, meaning that all government documents and proceedings are accessible in French. Further, Acadians are well-represented in government, where at least a dozen of the fifty-odd legislative assembly members are of French heritage.

Acadian influence is particularly strong in towns such as Campbellton. One of its three radio stations is French-speaking and another is mixed French and English. Of the two major television stations, one offers French and English, the other just French. Two of the six most popular daily papers (including papers from other cities such as Moncton and Saint John) are French. The legislative assembly member is Acadian. Even so, in places like Campbellton, the people, cultures, and languages are a mix of Acadian, English, Mi'kmaq, and other heritages. The town's festival events play down differences and celebrate events like the salmon run and the beginning of winter.

Rural Living in the Maritimes

While the cities have attracted heavy industry, natural resource companies, and high-tech and telecom sectors, rural areas in the maritimes retain a traditional flavor and a reliance on agriculture, fishing, and forestry. In many ways, small towns embody the ways of life that keep the provinces connected to the past. Throughout the provinces, tightly knit small towns vary in ethnic background and lifestyles.

On Prince Edward Island, small towns survive mainly on local businesses and seasonal employment. For instance, Montague, an eastern shore town of about two thousand people, has a workforce of almost eight hundred people but only about half of these people are employed full-time year-round. The rest are part-time or part-year workers, and their incomes are significantly lower than the provincial average. Agriculture, fishing, forestry, manufacturing, and retail jobs account for about half of the local economy. The unemployment rate in Montague is nearly 20 percent, well above the 13 percent rate of the province—an indication of a lack of full-time job opportunities. Despite the economic challenges, the town offers a range of attractions including a town park and playground, a curling club, an ice rink, and three nearby provincial parks.

In New Brunswick, rural towns often face similar challenges from a limited economy. For example, tiny Kedgwick in the northwest is made up of about twelve hundred people, nearly all of whom speak French. Nestled against the Appalachia Mountains, the town was originally built around logging. Today, less than 10 percent of the workforce still participates in logging. The construction industry has outpaced logging but there are nevertheless too few jobs. Unemployment has at times approached 30 percent. Despite the challenges, the people are known for their welcoming attitude to travelers who come to visit the beautiful natural surroundings.

Many of Nova Scotia's small towns thrive on the ocean and its offerings. Coastal villages' ability to embody the provincial identity can also promote tourism. "Along the waterfront," notes Mark Kurlansky in *Cod: A Biography of the Fish That Changed the World*, "the wooden-shingled houses are brick red, a color that originally came from mixing clay with cod-liver oil to protect the wood against the salt of the waterfront. It is the look of Nova Scotia—brick red wood, dark green pine, charcoal sea."[15] Ironically, attracting too many tourists is one of the easiest ways for postcard-perfect towns to lose their unique charm.

Coastal towns in Nova Scotia also balance tourism with other industries. Pictou, located on Northumberland Strait

■ *Traditionally dressed Acadian children enjoy a horse-drawn cart ride in rural New Brunswick.*

some 90 miles (150 kilometers) from Halifax, is home to about four thousand people. Originally a Scottish settlement, in the nineteenth century a gun battery protected the harbor, long a launching point for cargo and fishing ships, from enemies. During World War II the Pictou Shipyard was busy constructing Allied warships. Today, the historic shipyard is closed, though plans are afoot to reactivate it, and much of the economy relies on tourism (nearby Munroe's Island is a natural sanctuary with several wetland areas that draw eco-tourists), retail, manufacturing (the town is home to a knife-making plant), and construction. Roughly 10 percent of town residents still participate in fishing and agriculture-related industries.

■ *A replica of the* Hector, *a ship that brought Scottish settlers to Nova Scotia in 1773, is docked at Pictou Marina.*

Strengthening Education

Over the last forty years, the people of the maritimes have worked hard to strengthen their educational systems. Schools work to meet the diverse needs of their students, with many offering instruction in both English and French or emphasizing technology. Public schools in all three provinces cover children from kindergarten through twelfth grade. Schools across the provinces range in size and focus depending on the community.

Beechville Lakeside Timberlea Elementary School, part of the Halifax Regional School System, educates eight hundred students per year. The school offers French immersion as well as traditional subjects like math, history, and grammar. Children also learn about technology and class websites post children's work.

In rural Campbellton, New Brunswick, the school system handles the needs of a diverse regional population. The town is home to an English K-4 school, a French K-6, a mixed middle school, a French high school, and an English high school. Approximately 25 percent of the middle school pupils are native children from nearby Listiguj, Quebec, while the other 75 percent come from surrounding towns like McLeods to the east and Robinsonville and Upsalquitch to the west. The 75 percent are a mix of French and English ancestry, and immersion programs are provided. Students generally arrive on buses, and their traditional instruction is balanced by a one-hour activity period at the end of school during which students can learn sign language, calligraphy, chess, or other skills. Further, the school has its own radio station with student DJs who broadcast live afternoon request shows, favorites countdowns, and new music selections.

On Prince Edward Island, the rural setting means that many of the schools are consolidated, taking in children from surrounding areas in grades one to eight or nine. Most children generally attend a separate regional high school between ninth and twelfth grades. At Montague Regional High School, kids in grades 10 through 12 come from the surrounding coastal region. The high school is somewhat unique in the province in that it offers not only core studies in science, math, social studies, and English, but also vocational training in carpentry, motor vehicle repair, welding, and industrial arts.

Modern Provinces with a Rich Past

The people of the maritime provinces have a long, rich history in Canada. Their ancestors include some of the first native peoples on the continent and some of the earliest Europeans to settle in the region. This rich heritage is a part of everyday life, but it is also uniquely expressed through the arts, traditions, and festivities of the people throughout the provinces.

Arts and Culture

W ith diverse residents and a strong respect for the past, the maritime provinces are steeped in artistic and cultural traditions. Offerings range from traditional native sculptures to quirky museums (like the Prince Edward Island Potato Museum) to modern theater. The provinces are also home to some of Canada's most famous artists, actors, and writers. With thriving urban centers and authentic small towns, the maritime provinces are a wonderful place to experience arts and culture.

Halifax: Cultural Hub of the Maritimes

As the maritimes' largest city, Halifax is its cultural hub, with dozens of heritage organizations, museums, and historic sites. Halifax is the first stop for exciting nightlife, good music, rich history, and modern art. Because the city depends so much on the harbor, much of its best offerings are related to the ocean. The Maritime Museum of the Atlantic was recently built as part of the city's Waterfront Development Project. The museum shows documentaries on the Halifax Explosion, and the collections contain portions of Queen Victoria's barge, pieces brought up from local shipwrecks, and even artifacts from the ill-fated *Titanic.* Further, the museum has preserved the CSS *Acadia,* the only surviving ship to have served the Royal Canadian Navy in both world wars. Launched in 1913 to survey the Canadian coastline, *Acadia* is also the only vessel still afloat to have survived the catastrophic Halifax harbor explosion of 1917. She has been featured in a number of recent movies, including a 1996 film in which she played the luxury liner *Lusitania.* Research about shipping and shipwreck history is ongoing at the museum, making it one of the area's most interesting and unique attractions.

The past and the city's tie to the port are brought together, as well, in the monument at Pier 21. From the 1920s to the 1970s, Pier 21 was the landing point for more than 1 million immigrants, 100,000 refugees, and 3,000 children escaping war-torn Britain during World War II. In addition, 494,000

■ Where the *Titanic* Victims Are Buried

When the *Titanic* went down in the North Atlantic during the early hours of April 15, 1912, nearly all rescue and recovery operations were launched from Halifax. As a result, 150 of the recovered bodies are buried in the city, as well. The majority of these, some 121 graves, are within Fairview Cemetery. The popularity of the 1998 movie *Titanic* has helped to turn Fairview into one of Halifax's more unusual tourist attractions.

The film chronicled the sinking of the ship from the perspective of two lovers, Jack Dawson and Rose DeWitt Bukater. While the love story is fiction, Jack Dawson is based on a man buried in Fairview Cemetery at plot 227, marked simply "J Dawson." The man is Joseph Dawson, a former Royal Army Medical Corpsman on his way from Dublin, Ireland, to America to find work. Joseph joined the ship as a trimmer, a ship laborer who moves coal and freight on a ship to distribute the weight properly. Raised in deep poverty, Joseph had no lover aboard ship, but had left behind a sweetheart, Nellie Priest, the daughter of a friend. Joseph's body was never claimed, and he was interred at Fairview Cemetery, though notice of his death eventually reached relatives in Ireland.

■ *Halifax's Fairview Cemetery attracts tourists to its Titanic section.*

Canadian troops passed over Pier 21 on their way to war. To-day, Pier 21 is a National Historic Site, an emotional monument to immigrants, displaced persons, and soldiers. The site's offerings include immigration papers, passports, and ships' menus from the immigration years. An examination hall and customs office where immigrants were inspected and where they presented papers have been faithfully re-created. The monument reminds tourists of the challenges immigrants faced throughout the century and the home that Canada has become for millions looking for a better life.

As the most diverse large city in the maritime provinces, Halifax honors its multiethnic heritage. The city has the largest black population in the three provinces, and it is home to the Black Cultural Centre, a heritage attraction that opened in 1983. The Centre chronicles the history of blacks' coming to Nova Scotia and New Brunswick and discusses connections to the Underground Railroad that ran slaves from the United States to safety in Canada. It also tells the stories of some of the most prominent black heroes, including that of famous Nova Scotia boxer Sam Langford. After moving to Massachusetts at age fourteen, Langford fought out of Boston and was known as the Boston Terror. He became so good that boxing officials who feared his prowess refused to allow him to fight

■ *More than a million immigrants were once processed at Halifax's Pier 21, now a National Historic Site.*

for the world title, though he held the English, Mexican, and Spanish titles. In 1917, an injury blinded him in one eye. He fought for another seven years until he was completely blind. The center proudly displays similar stories of other heroes to schoolchildren, members of the community, and tourists.

Finally, Halifax is the maritime center for fine art. The Art Gallery of Nova Scotia is the oldest, largest, and best-loved art gallery in the maritime provinces. It is home to approximately ten thousand pieces, including thousands of paintings and sculptures. The gallery focuses in particular on artists with ties to Nova Scotia, and its offerings range from the contemporary to the historic. Recent exhibitions have highlighted the work of Hantsport sculptor Colleen Wolstenholme, whose works range from jewelry pieces to body-sized pieces. Beyond art and sculpture, the gallery participates in the community, offering educational programs to schools and community members. The Early Childhood Program, for instance, offers daycare children ages three to five a chance to participate in hands-on painting, sculpting, and drawing activities. Other programs employ multimedia presentations to engage kids of all ages during guided tours.

Soulful Saint John

As the largest city in New Brunswick, Saint John is home to some of the province's most thriving artistic and cultural venues. Much of the artistic work is coordinated under the New Brunswick Arts Council, an organization formed in 1979 to bring performing and visual artists together and promote them throughout the city and province. The council's main goals are to provide residents quality live performance and artistic presentations, offer students access to artistic presentations they would not have otherwise, and provide a network for artists in the province. The council pushed its mandate into new territory in 2002 by hosting its first annual Festival of the Arts. Though based in Saint John, the council hosted the event in the capital city of Fredericton and attracted top performers and artists from around the province, including the Atlantic Ballet Company, the Saint John String Quartet, and visual artists Peggy Smith and Paul Healey, among others. Though just a one-day event for now, the council hopes to increase artistic awareness and promote artists' work across the province through such occasions.

Beyond being the coordinating center for much of New Brunswick's art, Saint John is also home to strong performing arts groups. Established in 1990, the Saint John Theatre Company is made up of community-based volunteers who put on three main stage plays per year as well as dinner theater, play readings, and second-stage productions. Productions have included well-known works like *The Diary of Anne Frank, Death of a Salesman,* and *The Woman in Black.* But the company also works to support local writers and artists—its 2003 Second Stage season included five original works by New Brunswick artists. Beyond theatre performances, the company conducts a community outreach program that reaches students in their classrooms or brings them into dress rehearsals to increase their interaction with the arts and encourage them to be lifetime artistic supporters.

In addition to artistic support, Saint John is home to natural and historical venues that keep the proud New Brunswick past alive and remind residents and tourists of the area's unique natural heritage. One of the best-known and most popular attractions is Reversing Falls, where the Bay of Fundy's extraordinarily high tides create fascinating natural

■ *One of the Saint John Theatre Company's most successful productions was* The Diary of Anne Frank.

effects. The south-facing opening of the Bay of Fundy receives high tides much like a funnel—water comes through a wide opening, then is forced through an ever narrower and shallower river, causing changes in the water's current. Eventually, low tide waters begin to retract, but high tide waters coming in clash with the retracting water, creating waves. Many people visit the site at least twice during a day to see the full effect.

Residents and tourists can connect with Saint John's past at the Carleton Martello Tower. The tower, now a National Historic Site, was built in 1812 to guard the land and sea approaches to the city. It was used from 1859 to 1866 to fight off the Fenian raids (an Irish uprising in Canada), in World War I to hold deserters from the Canadian army, and as an intelligence and antiaircraft post in World War II. The tower itself is a circular, stone, two-floor building; inside is a restored powder magazine, barracks, and two upper levels added during World War II. Guides lead people on tours throughout the day and provide background information. On days without fog, the strategic value of the tower is easy to see—the structure sits on one of the highest points in the city, and the outstanding view from the top stretches wide and far.

■ *The Carleton Martello Tower overlooking Saint John has been transformed from a military asset to a tourist attraction.*

Charlottetown's Arts and Theater

Charlottetown is noted throughout Canada as an artistic and cultural center. The Confederation Centre of the Arts is the hub of artistic activity in the town and perhaps in all of Prince Edward Island. The venue hosts concerts by acts like Wave, the popular Canadian pop music band, and world-class fiddler Natalie MacMaster. Further, the center hosts major artistic showings, like the 2003 exhibition of Saskatoon-based artist Alison Norlen's charcoal sketches. The center's art gallery also hosts adult and children's art classes.

Perhaps above all else, the center is known for hosting the Charlottetown Festival from May to mid-October. During those months, the festival puts on the largest assortment of musical and comedy plays in all of Canada. It also specializes in bringing new works to the stage. Begun in 1965, the festival has commissioned and put on more than sixty productions, ranging from *Dracula—A Chamber Musical,* which tells the story of the creepy vampire count, to *Fire,* the story of two Deep South brothers who fall in love with and marry the same girl.

Not surprisingly, the single most popular Charlottetown Festival play has been an adaptation of Lucy Maud Montgomery's childhood classic, *Anne of Green Gables.* First performed on July 7, 1965, the play has drawn more than 2 million viewers over its almost four-decade run. Montgomery's moving novel, which was first published in 1908, recounts the experiences of Anne Shirley, an orphan mistakenly sent to a Prince Edward Island farm family that had wanted a boy. "Perhaps no other region in North America is so strongly identified with a hundred-year-old literary heroine," notes *New York Times* writer James Ledbetter. He goes on to say about the novel:

> It strongly appeals to preteenage girls around the globe, who flock here in zestful hordes. Scuttlebutt holds that not all tourists—especially the Japanese, whose national school curriculum includes *Anne of Green Gables*—recognize that Anne is a fictional character. Who could blame them? Anne is the island's omnipresent genie: you can buy dolls in her likeness at gas stations, she has her own line of soap and soft drinks and until recently license plates in the province featured the spunky redhead.[16]

Often disparaged by critics as a simple children's story, the book is full of strong feminist undertones, and it has brought laughter to children and adults for nearly one hundred years and has spawned numerous plays, a musical, and television

■ *The Green Gables House, grounds, and farm outbuildings portray the Victorian setting of L.M. Montgomery's beloved novel.*

adaptations. The legacy of *Anne* lives on in Prince Edward Island. The house that inspired the setting of *Anne*, Green Gables House, is now part of the Prince Edward Island National Historic Park. It welcomes hundreds of thousands of tourists per year who come to learn about Montgomery's influence on the island and the effect of the book on the world. Visitors are free to take trails through the hollows and woods that inspired many of the scenes in Montgomery's book. A major tourist draw and the island's greatest cultural legacy to the world, *Anne* continues to be a vital part of the island.

Like its sister cities, Charlottetown is also a key provincial venue for connecting with the past. The city hosts the annual Festival of the Fathers, a celebration of the 1864 Charlottetown Conference that launched the drive to Confederation. Though the conference initially caused concern among islanders hesitant to join the confederation, it was a turning point both for the nation and the island. Today, the festival is held at the end of August for four days. Actors reenact the delegates' arrival to the conference and bring other meetings and proceedings to life. The reenactments are supplemented by concerts in the park, performances for children, a family picnic, and tours through historic parts of Charlottetown.

■ The Island's Own *Anne of Green Gables*

Born November 30, 1874, in Clifton (now New London), Prince Edward Island, Lucy Maud Montgomery shared much in common with her world-famous orphan Anne Shirley. Montgomery's mother died of tuberculosis when Lucy was only two, and she was sent to Cavendish, a nearby farming town on the Gulf of St. Lawrence, to be raised by her grandparents. She studied at Charlottetown's Prince of Wales College and Halifax's Dalhousie University, and was writing professionally by her mid-twenties. Her love of the island's beauty and people led her to write a novel, *Anne of Green Gables*, which was rejected by several publishers before being published in 1908 when Montgomery was thirty-four.

In 1911 Montgomery married and moved to Ontario but she continued to mine her experiences on Prince Edward Island for later works. These included six sequels to *Anne of Green Gables* that followed Anne Shirley's development as an adult. Although none of Montgomery's subsequent works became so popular or beloved as her first novel, she was a prolific writer who penned some two dozen novels, including two for adults, as well as poems, short stories, and journals. Upon her death in Toronto on April 24, 1942, she left behind voluminous diary entries that have been published in four "selected journals" since 1985.

Montgomery remains a major presence on Prince Edward Island in part because the provincial government is a joint owner, along with heirs Ruth Macdonald and David Macdonald, of the licensing authority that controls all use of *Anne of Green Gables* images and trademarks, including Green Gables House. Almost one hundred individuals and businesses have been licensed to sell Anne-inspired jewelry, dolls, sculptures, clothing, organic potting soil, maple syrup, wooden birdhouses, gift wrap, and more. Scholars also keep Montgomery in the spotlight through research, international conferences, and other work at Prince Edward Island University's ten-year-old L.M. Montgomery Institute.

■ *Writer L.M. Montgomery created Prince Edward Island's most memorable fictional character.*

Native Arts and Culture

The Loyalist and French heritages are hardly the only things to celebrate in the three provinces. Though their numbers are small when compared with the rest of the population, aboriginal peoples make important contributions through their artistic and cultural expressions. Mi'kmaq and other First Nations celebrate the long history they have in the Atlantic region, even while they grapple with the difficult past they have had with European settlers and the challenges they find today.

On Lennox Island, a small portion of Prince Edward Island set aside for the Mi'kmaq, artistic expression not only connects people to their heritage, it is a lively business. For instance, one of the most prominent businesses among the Mi'kmaq is the Indian Art & Craft of North America store, run by Charlie and Doreen Sark. The store offers Mi'kmaq crafts, such as figurines and baskets made of white ash. On the side, Charlie has started another business selling figurines of Glooskap, the legendary giant credited by the Mi'kmaq for creating humans. Charlie uses his business to help other Mi'kmaq. He sends his workers

■ *Crafts such as carving and painting figurines thrive throughout the maritimes.*

■ Mi'kmaq Artist Randy Simon Merges Traditional and Modern

Mi'kmaq artist Randy Simon was born a member of the Big Cove First Nation in eastern New Brunswick and has been an artist and sculptor for as long as he can remember. In his mid-thirties, Simon is becoming one of the most recognized Mi'kmaq artists in the region.

Simon draws inspiration for his work from the oral traditions and legends of the Mi'kmaq. Simon notes that many such stories have been lost over the years, while many others are in danger of not surviving the next couple of generations. Thus, in his sculptures, he works to represent the stories he sees being threatened. His sculptures tend to show natural or mythical animals, each coming from a story Simon hopes to preserve.

Simon's work has been increasingly recognized in New Brunswick and throughout the region. He is mentioned repeatedly in native publications, and his work has been shown in Fredericton and is sold online and in stores across the province, sometimes retailing for twelve hundred dollars. A professional sculptor for only about five years, his popularity seems sure to spread throughout the country.

to Summerside where the company Cavendish Figurines, a manufacturer of *Anne of Green Gables* figures, trains the employees in molding and painting figures. Charlie's work has brought jobs to the reserve, and the store he jointly runs increases native pride and interaction with outsiders.

In other areas of the provinces, native artists and crafts makers are influencing the culture. The Nova Scotia Museum, a collection of twenty-five museums across Nova Scotia, devotes an entire heritage collection to the Mi'kmaq. The collection includes more than eight hundred portraits, paintings, and pieces of rock art collected from Mi'kmaq artists over the years. The museum also provides historical information on the Mi'kmaq. In New Brunswick, Mi'kmaq and Maliseet artistic and cultural influence has increased significantly over the last twenty years, leading the province to take a more active role in dispersing native art and providing native historical information. The Aboriginal Affairs division of the provincial government now publishes native histories online and in print, and native groups across the province have increased their artistic offerings on their lands and in shops and museums.

Small-Town Arts and Crafts

Heritage and cultural celebrations in small towns throughout the provinces are not as large or grand as those in the big cities, but they are vital nevertheless to the people. Festivals, arts and crafts, and shops devoted to works like *Anne of Green Gables* are just a few of the small-town offerings commonly found in the maritimes. Other offerings celebrate the fishing heritage and the richness of French and European culture.

In the tiny French-dominated town of Kedgwick, New Brunswick, the principal attraction is the Kedgwick Forestry Museum and Campsite. The site re-creates a 1930s logging site, and visitors can camp for days at a time. Guided tours of woodsman camps give tourists a taste of what working in forestry was really like during its heyday. Multimedia presentations explore the history of Kedgwick forestry, and the brilliant outdoor surroundings are attractions alone for many others.

In Nova Scotia, Berwick in the Annapolis Valley boasts that it is the apple capital of Canada. Home to just over two thousand people, Berwick also boasts a proud tradition of community fun. The town features the Berwick Apple Capital Interpretive Centre, a heritage spot that preserves relics of the town's most important industry of the last one hundred years. Beyond that, the late-summer Gala Days festival draws residents for parades, casino night, concerts, fireworks, a strongman competition, and barbecues, among other festivities. The event is the town's most important celebration—a true community-bonding experience for all who participate.

Souris (the name is pronounced like the English name "Surrey"), Prince Edward Island, is a small east-coast town originally settled by the Acadians. It is now an important fishing port, and its connection to the sea is crucial to its festivities. The year's big seaside event is Souris Regatta Days. The annual July "Celebration of the Sea" event draws residents and tourists to boat races, recipe competitions, entertainment, wood carving competitions, and a sand sculpting contest. The town is also home to the Basin Head Fishery Museum, a venue showing the boats and photographs that explain the lifestyle of a fishing town. A boardwalk leads people to a pristine white sand beach.

The land itself remains a major attraction in Nova Scotia, as guidebook author Wayne Curtis notes:

> In the end, what impresses me most about Nova Scotia is this: I'll finish up a ramble on a back road somewhere and finally pull up to the main highway. And what I'll see is this:

■ Sherbrooke: A Village-Sized Museum

On the eastern shore of Nova Scotia is tiny Sherbrooke Village, about half of which is a historic section managed as part of the Nova Scotia Museum. The town's history is marked particularly by an 1860s gold rush that caused a town boom. When the gold rush passed, the town got involved in forestry and even returned to mining during parts of the twentieth century.

But perhaps nothing has been as successful as the tourist haven it is now. Sherbrooke Village depicts the typical lifestyle of a Nova Scotia village from 1860 to the World War I years. Of the eighty buildings, twenty-five are open to the public, making the village the largest Nova Scotia Museum site.

While there are several similar villages in the other provinces (and, elsewhere in Nova Scotia, the largest historic reconstruction project in Canada, at Fortress of Louisbourg National Historic Park), Sherbrooke Village is unique in that people still live in many of the homes. The paid-admission village offers a functioning blacksmith shop, general store, boatbuilding shop, house tours, and more. Events are held throughout the year, including the famed Old-Fashioned Christmas held each year at the end of November. Festivities include a Victorian tea, home tours, Christmas concerts, and craft making. Other events are held throughout the year, and the village welcomes visitors wholeheartedly.

■ *Big-wheeled bicycles and other examples of late-nineteenth century technology are alive and well at Sherbrooke Village.*

nothing. No cars in either direction. If this were New England, I'd be tapping my fingers to the turn signal while awaiting an opening between RVs and impatient cars. Not here. There's still a sense of remoteness, of being surrounded by big space and a profound history. More than once I had the fleeting sense that I was visiting New England, but 60 or 70 years ago, well before anyone referred to tourism as an industry.[17]

Culture and Economy

The maritime people's love of their culture and past is often at odds with modern developments. While thousands of land developers and tourists have discovered the beauty and joy of coastal living and have boosted the economy, many are reluctant to give up their decades-old lifestyles and the "good life" they enjoy. Many of today's challenges center on modernizing the provinces further and improving and preserving their services. But even while government and communities work at these issues, others wish for greater independence and the traditional lifestyles they have always enjoyed.

Current Challenges

O ver the past four decades the maritimes have worked hard to catch up to the rest of Canada in economic development. The economies of all three provinces have grown stronger in recent years, even as other provincial economies have dipped. But keeping the momentum going and providing adequate education and health care services are challenges for all three provinces. Shifts in the world economy could still prove dangerous to the region, and overall employment in the maritimes remains somewhat below the rest of Canada. Sharply rising health care costs threaten to overwhelm the budgets in all three provinces, and finding the funds to continue to improve educational systems remains a challenge.

Within this framework, government officials are aware of the delicate balance that exists between the urge to modernize and the need to respect the simple, traditional lifestyles many residents of the maritimes love. The maritime provinces' greatest challenge in the near future may be securing economic prosperity for all citizens without sacrificing what one writer calls the "extraordinary combination of history, wilderness, and surprise [found] in these beautiful, out-of-the-mainstream, thinly populated provinces."[18]

Shoring Up the Economy

The maritime provinces have achieved remarkable economic success in the last several years. New Brunswick's economy grew at 4.2 percent in 2002, well ahead of the country's 2.2

percent, and Saint John's economy led all Canadian cities in job growth. Prince Edward Island has seen similar success. Since 1996, more than seven thousand jobs have been added to its economy, ranging from traditional jobs such as lobster fishing to scientific research, easing unemployment figures across the economy. In response, new home construction jumped 50 percent from 2001 to 2002. In Nova Scotia, the successful economy has brought the unemployment rate down under 10 percent. With increased revenues and better management, the government has successfully balanced its budget.

■ *Lobstering remains a profitable livelihood even as the fishing industry has experienced hard times.*

In spite of these successes, the provinces have much to do economically. The unemployment rates in all three provinces are well above the recent Canadian average of 7 to 8 percent and compare poorly to provinces such as Manitoba and Alberta, where rates are just above 5 percent. A number of initiatives are under way to address the problem of ongoing unemployment in the maritime provinces and to continue to strengthen the regional economy. The maritimes have low real estate and labor costs, and the monetary exchange rate makes it advantageous for American companies to relocate to Canadian provinces. These factors have helped promote further modernization and development.

Nova Scotia is moving rapidly to bring in high-tech, manufacturing, and resource industries. Halifax is a prime draw for many companies because one in every four of its workers holds a postsecondary degree—the highest percentage among major Canadian cities. With eleven degree-granting institutions in Nova Scotia, the province is positioned to take advantage of an increasingly complex global economy. Growth has been particularly strong in the telecom and teleservice sectors. In 1998, Convergys opened the largest teleservice center in Atlantic Canada. It has since hired and trained twelve hundred employees. Register.com followed that in 2002, announcing that it would open a center employing more than three hundred people.

Meanwhile, manufacturing has seen renewed emphasis with new plants producing helicopter parts, computer components, and other products. The Sable Island natural gas reserves are also starting to pay off. "With both offshore and onshore facilities for producing and processing natural gas," notes *Canada 2000* author Wayne C. Thompson, "it is the largest industrial undertaking in the province's history and Canada's biggest construction project entering the twenty-first century. Delivery of gas began in 1999, with New England as the principal market."[19]

From Call Centers to Aerospace

New Brunswick has focused on maintaining its foundation of resource industries, manufacturing, and construction while expanding its knowledge-based offerings. Like Nova Scotia, New Brunswick has recently been successful in luring teleservice companies to the area. Moncton and Fredericton are home to

■ A Unique Answer to the Fishing Crash

In the early 1990s, the Atlantic fishing industry suffered a severe blow when the government suspended commercial cod fishing, thus crippling many fishing companies in the maritime provinces and Newfoundland. But a new fish-raising method, called aquaculture, may help save the fishing industry. Aquaculture is similar to farming or ranching. Fish are grown in large tanks or cages, fattened until they reach a marketable weight, then harvested and either processed or sold fresh. Special care is taken to control diseases and to prevent farm-raised fish, which may be genetically modified, from escaping into the wild.

The aquaculture industry is booming in the region. New Brunswick garnered $282 million in aquaculture sales in 2000, while Nova Scotia pulled in $44 million and Prince Edward Island $29 million. Colleges are incorporating aquaculture as a field of study in their curricula, and farms and colleges are studying techniques to reduce costs and improve yield. Among the fish raised by aquaculture in the maritimes are salmon, trout, eels, striped bass, and shellfish.

The industry has not outstripped traditional fishing just yet—the old way brought in $1.7 billion to Atlantic Canada in 2000. But the new method appears to be the future. Jim Crawford of Nova Scotia, a former fisherman turned aquaculturist, told *Maclean's*, "As long as we look after the environment, this industry has unlimited potential."

■ *Fish pens like the one at this New Brunswick aquaculture facility provide an alternative to conventional fishing operations.*

United Parcel Service call centers that employ more than one thousand people. EDS and other companies have put in call centers in New Brunswick, as well. Frank McKenna, the former New Brunswick premier who helped launch the call center revolution, gushes, "The sky is the limit. This industry could double in size and still not be anywhere near saturation."[20] Beyond those successes, New Brunswick is working to shore up traditional mining, fishing, and forestry industries. Exports of goods have doubled over the last ten years, and New Brunswick has seen a new sugar refining factory open in Saint John and a new plastics facility in Minto.

Prince Edward Island is boosting its economy by seeking to attract a variety of companies, from manufacturing to food processing. In 2002, an aerospace company announced it would open a facility on Prince Edward Island for engineering and research and development. Beyond those successes, Prince Edward Island's Confederation Bridge has pushed tourism higher, with more than 1 million visitors coming to the island each year.

Aggressive government marketing campaigns, combined with the maritimes' low real estate and labor costs, have helped to turn around the area's traditional struggling economies. More jobs and new residents are welcome developments though they can put new pressures on government services and social programs.

Combining Government Forces

The maritime provinces have always shared common interests due to their similar cultures, geography, and economies. Before confederation, there were calls to unify the provinces under one government. While there are few advocates of such a plan today, the increasing challenges to economic development, health care services, and other social programs have created collective burdens on the provinces. In response, they have looked to join forces and streamline their governments. One of the newest programs is the Council of Atlantic Premiers, created in 2000. This unique organization joins the premiers of all three maritime provinces with the premier of Newfoundland to pursue a healthier regional economy, higher-quality public services, and more affordable health care.

The results, thus far, have been impressive. The Council of Atlantic Premiers has helped initiate trade missions in which

■ *The premiers of the four Atlantic provinces are, from left to right, John Hamm (N.S.), Roger Grimes (Newfoundland), Pat Binns (P.E.I.), and Bernard Lord (N.B.).*

representatives of more than 150 Atlantic companies visited with key industry and government personnel in New England and in the U.S. South. These trade missions have sparked increased investment and created new business partnerships, contributing to the maritimes' growing economy in recent years. The council has also encouraged investment in information technologies that have improved the quality of health care across the region. It has established a central location in Halifax for all organ and tissue donations, increasing the speed with which needed operations can be conducted. In education, the council has boosted several regional organizations that provide scholarships and infrastructure support to colleges and students.

For the future, the council is working aggressively to enhance the region's relationship with the United States and other important trading partners. In health care, it plans to establish a drug review board that will provide practical recommendations on adding drugs to health care plans. In education, the council is starting programs aimed at identifying struggling readers, improving overall literacy, and connecting schools in remote areas to the Internet.

While the council and related organizations are working on solutions for the regions, the individual provinces still have unique challenges to meet. One of the most perplexing is the health care funding problem, and each province is working toward a separate solution.

Who Will Pay for Residents' Health?

The Canadian system of publicly funded health care guarantees basic benefits for all residents, though certain specialized services require personal payments. The federal government grants provinces money each year to cover the benefits guaranteed by federal law. Provinces also supply their own funding for additional programs and infrastructure. Federal and provincial funds are generated from income and other taxes. The problem? Health care costs are currently rising at 10 to 15 percent per year, easily outstripping the federal and provincial revenue growth needed to pay for them. The most dire commentators say that eventually guaranteed health care will

■ Among the Aboriginal Cultures Today

Prince Edward Island is home to about one thousand aboriginals, Nova Scotia to more than twelve thousand, and New Brunswick to more than ten thousand. Mainly Mi'kmaq and Maliseet, they were participants—unlike many of the First Nations of central and western Canada—in certain pre-confederation treaties known as the Maritime Peace and Friendship Treaties. Signed between 1725 and 1779, these were essentially agreements on peace and trade. The Royal Proclamation of 1763, however, converted the treaties to land agreements and set aside native lands that prohibited white settlers. Today, First Nations are challenging the terms of the treaties, and the provinces are working to resolve land claims.

Life on the native reserves today is a mix of the traditional and the modern. On Prince Edward Island the Mi'kmaq are allotted four small reserve areas, including Lennox Island. Many natives are involved in arts and crafts industries, and people like the Sarks are working to invigorate business opportunities for aboriginals. In New Brunswick, there are fifteen First Nations communities, ranging in population size from little more than 150 to several thousand. Services and job opportunities include elementary schools, fire and ambulance services, and small computer training and support businesses. Nova Scotia is home to thirteen First Nations groups.

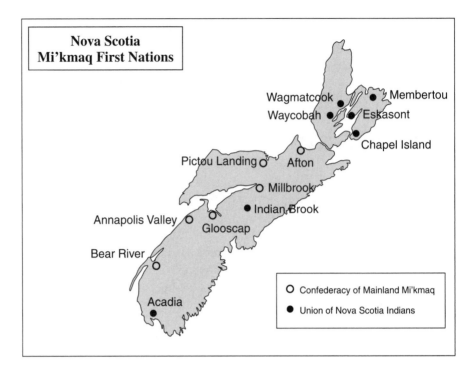

**Nova Scotia
Mi'kmaq First Nations**

Wagmatcook · · Membertou
Waycobah · · Eskasont
Chapel Island
Pictou Landing ○ ○ Afton
○ Millbrook
· Indian Brook
Annapolis Valley ○ ○
Glooscap
Bear River
○
Acadia
·

○ Confederacy of Mainland Mi'kmaq
· Union of Nova Scotia Indians

be unaffordable, pointing to provinces like Alberta that have sought to reduce coverage in order to contain costs.

The maritime provinces are hoping to avoid benefit cuts even as their aging populations present a major challenge. In New Brunswick, for example, the senior citizens who make up 13 percent of the population are the fastest growing segment, and the province expects the number of people over sixty-five to increase 38 percent by 2016. The cost of prescription drugs, a chief factor in rising health care costs, is growing annually at 13 percent. This particularly hurts senior citizens because they typically take far more medications than younger people.

Nova Scotia is seeing similar growth among its aging population—14 percent of the population is over sixty-five, and that number is expected to rise. Within recent years the province has put tens of millions of dollars into home care and long-term care programs, even though the federal government does not reimburse provinces for such senior programs. In Prince Edward Island, the public remains generally pleased with health care, but chronic diseases like cancer, heart disease, and diabetes are disturbingly high. This is partly due to the growing numbers of residents who are over sixty-five and thus are being diagnosed with more of these problems.

The provinces believe that providing adequate funding for health care pays off in the long run by keeping residents healthier as they age. To meet health care goals New Brunswick recently put more than $14 million into recruiting additional nurses and doctors. As a result 95 percent of all New Brunswick residents have access to a family care physician—the highest percentage of any province—and the ratio of nurses to residents exceeds the national average by 25 percent. The province has also established community health centers to increase rural residents' access to care. In Nova Scotia, a balanced budget has allowed the province to increase funding for health care, meaning that hospitals can spend less time fighting for money and more time recruiting doctors and nurses. Finally, Prince Edward Island is working to curb the incidence of chronic illnesses by banning smoking from public places and launching educational programs related to diet and exercise.

Toward a Sustainable Environment

The maritimes rely heavily on the land's limited natural resources, including its trees, fish, soil, and water. In the past, poor management has led to problems such as deforestation, overfishing along the coast and in the bays, and pesticide contamination of drinking water supplies. The provinces now face the challenge of developing sustainable approaches that balance often-conflicting demands for jobs, recreation, and scenic beauty.

As with other issues, each province has particular challenges to grapple with, ranging from cleaning up groundwater to managing land use. Prince Edward Island's history is marked by environmental conflicts. The rapid growth of farms led to widespread deforestation. Further, farms were not always managed well, and rain runoff caused soil erosion, contaminated groundwater, and even killed large numbers of fish.

Today, Prince Edward Island is taking aim at several of these problems. It has spent millions of dollars on soil and water conservation, mandated three-year crop rotation cycles for farmers, and promoted the growing of mixed fruit and vegetable crops, ranging from strawberries to pumpkins, in smaller-scale, less water-intensive operations. It has eliminated cattle access to streams, preventing waste matter from polluting groundwater, and it has increased reforestation projects. In recent years, the province has hired a freshwater ecologist to study the problem of farm runoff killing large numbers of freshwater fish. The province is educating landowners about

■ *By late June strawberry fields in Prince Edward Island's Queens County are usually ready for picking.*

water management practices and pesticide use. To improve drinking water, it is upgrading and expanding water treatment and sewer plants. Further, to reduce soil misuse, the government is tightening standards on buffer zones and conservation tillage, meaning that landowners must keep certain lands untilled to prevent water and wind erosion.

Similar conservationist efforts are proving to be just as effective elsewhere in the maritimes. In New Brunswick, land misuse is an ongoing concern. Forests have often been knocked down and not properly replaced, and industries and towns have encroached upon sensitive environmental areas. New zoning requirements and land use planning reforms have begun to improve the situation in both urban and rural areas. Efforts in Nova Scotia have focused on reducing waste, encouraging recycling, and improving water quality. Federal and provincial cooperation has produced significant funding to upgrade provincial water treatment plants. The province has recently hired fourteen new hydrologists to study water practices and improve water management.

While the maritime provinces are working to address concerns about social services, health care, and the environment, other current challenges relate to cultural and political issues.

Stemming Soil Erosion on Prince Edward Island

Prince Edward Island's number one environmental problem is soil erosion. In shallow rivers, the bottoms are composed of loose sediment. While some loose sediment is natural in the island's rivers, much of it winds up there through land misuse. Excessive sediment blocks sunlight that allows plants and fish to grow, and it slows rivers that carry needed water to different parts of the province. Finally, sediment dumped into the ocean can carry toxic chemicals that can devastate oyster and fish stocks and hurt the insects that fish survive on.

The chief cause of soil erosion on Prince Edward Island is farmland that abuts rivers. One-third of the provincial land is farmland, and many tons of soil per square acre can be washed into rivers if soil is not managed well. For years, many farmers have plowed to the edge of rivers and then left their topsoil bare during the winter. Storms and winds move the topsoil down into the rivers, causing the most severe problems. Further, farm productivity is lost as valuable, nutrient-rich topsoil pours into rivers.

The province's response thus far has been to create buffer zones—areas that farmers must leave untilled between farmland and water. The program has shown promising results, reducing major fish kills, although environmentalists say that further improvements are needed.

■ *Farms on the shores of Prince Edward Island's New London Bay need to protect against soil erosion.*

Cultural Truce in New Brunswick

New Brunswick shares with neighboring Quebec many common traits, including large French-speaking populations. Unlike Quebec, however, New Brunswick has enjoyed more cultural stability and has not had to confront a separatist movement like the one favored by many French-speaking Quebecois. Partly this is because in the 1960s, when New Brunswick's Acadian population expressed fears about seeing their culture overwhelmed by the larger English presence, the Acadians demanded language and education rights. And they got them. In 1969, for example, New Brunswick passed a language law that recognized the equality of English and French in the legislature, courts, and public service, making New Brunswick the only officially bilingual province in Canada.

Today, New Brunswick is more evenly divided between French and English speakers than any other province (Quebec is about 85 percent French-speaking), and the mix is generally harmonious. As *Boston Globe* writer Patricia Harris notes,

■ *Acadian flags remain a popular symbol of unity among New Brunswick's French-speaking population.*

> While the people of New Brunswick's Acadian Peninsula are proud to have survived an attempt at cultural extinction, their comfortable historical remove lets them concentrate more on celebrating what they preserved than

on fumbling over history. They are quick to break into a dance at the sound of a fiddle, laugh heartily at a corny old joke, or pull over to the side of the road to feast on a patch of wild blueberries.[21]

There are French schools, a French university, signs in French, French radio and TV stations, and numerous French and bilingual politicians. And though there can be cultural differences and tensions, these are far less divisive than those in Quebec. In part, the Acadians in New Brunswick consider themselves separate from the French in Quebec or other parts of the country. Though they both come from the same roots, the Acadians never received much French government support—in essence, the community came to rely on itself, especially during and after the expulsion. So the causes taken up by the Quebecois do not always translate into major concerns in New Brunswick.

Many residents consider the bilingual nature of the province to be one of its greatest economic strengths. In the push to bring call centers and other industries to the province, government leaders have marketed the province's bilingual strengths with great success. Air Canada and Royal

■ *Rolling fields and pastoral woodlands provide prime birdwatching opportunities on Prince Edward Island.*

Bank are just two of the companies that looked on New Brunswick's bilingual strength favorably and placed phone banks there.

Balancing the Traditional with the Modern

The maritime provinces have typically been separated from the rest of Canada and the world, in part by geography. But as the regional economy grows and people discover the area's natural beauty, tourists and workers are flocking to the maritimes. These new faces threaten to change old lifestyles and gobble up limited land space, forcing the maritimes to balance the desire to welcome newcomers with the need to preserve its unique culture.

On Prince Edward Island, for example, the booming tourism industry during the summer threatens to overwhelm the rural nature of the island. As the most densely populated province per square mile, Prince Edward Island has limited undeveloped areas. The 30 percent jump in tourism that the province experienced with the opening of Confederation Bridge put additional pressures on development, meaning that more hotels, golf courses, and tourist attractions are being built. Year-round residents complain that once-rural routes are now plagued by traffic jams, and residents have begun to oppose proposals for theme parks and other tourist-related development in environmentally and culturally sensitive areas.

New Brunswick and Nova Scotia face similar debates about how best to balance new development with respect for the maritime heritage. The issue is especially difficult in rural areas where the economy is still stagnant and the population slowly dwindles as young people leave for the city to take jobs or attend university. Special tax incentives for economic development in rural areas can help, as can increased attention to extending the reach of government programs and services. Many of these programs are in the formative stage, and managing the balance of sustainable growth while preserving a rural heritage is sure to be an ongoing challenge.

The maritime provinces are changing rapidly in today's global economy. They are working to keep pace with the rest of Canada and to solve their most pressing social problems. As a people that have overcome wars, natural and human-made disasters, and ethnic tensions, they appear ready to stand and meet the challenges ahead.

Facts About
the Maritime
Provinces

Government

- Form: Parliamentary system with federal and provincial levels

- Highest official: Premier, who administers provincial legislation and regulations

- Capitals: Fredericton, N.B.; Halifax, N.S.; Charlottetown, P.E.I.

- Entered confederation: New Brunswick and Nova Scotia on July 1, 1867 (two of the four original provinces); Prince Edward Island on July 1, 1873 (seventh province)

Land

- Area: New Brunswick: 28,355 square miles (73,439 square kilometers); 0.7% of total land of Canada, ranking eleventh in size among the thirteen provinces and territories; Nova Scotia: 21,425 square miles (55,491 square kilometers); 0.6%; twelfth-largest; Prince Edward Island: 2,185 square miles (5,659 square kilometers); 0.05%; smallest province

- National parks: New Brunswick: Fundy, Kouchibouguac; Nova Scotia: Cape Breton Islands, Kejimkujik; Prince Edward Island: Prince Edward Island

- Highest point: Mount Carleton, N.B., 2,690 feet (820 meters)

- Largest lake: Bras d'Or Lake, 424 square miles (1,099 square kilometers)

- Other major lakes: Lake Rossignol, N.S.; Grand Lake, N.B.

- Longest river: Saint John, 428 miles (673 kilometers)

- Other major rivers: Annapolis, St. Mary's, Medway, Mersey, Shubenacadie, and Margaree (N.S.); Miramichi, Restigouche, Nepisiguit, Salmon, St. Croix, and Tobique (N.B.)

- Largest island: Cape Breton, N.S., 3,981 square miles (10,311 square kilometers); 18th-largest island in Canada

- Time zones: Atlantic

- Geographical extremes: approximately 43° N to 48° N latitude; 69° W to 60° W longitude

People

- Population: New Brunswick: 729,498 (2001 census), ranking 8th among provinces and territories and representing 2.4% of Canada's total population of 30,007,094; Nova Scotia: 908,077, 7th, 3.0%; Prince Edward Island: 135,294, 10th, 0.5%

- Annual growth rate: New Brunswick: −1.2% from 1996 to 2001, ranking 10th in growth rate among provinces and territories; Nova Scotia: −0.1%, 8th; Prince Edward Island: 0.5%, 7th

- Location: New Brunswick: 49% urban; 51% rural; Nova Scotia: 55% urban; 45% rural; Prince Edward Island: 44% urban; 56% rural

- Predominant heritages: British, French (34% in New Brunswick; 4% in Nova Scotia, and 4% in Prince Edward Island), aboriginal

- Largest ethnic groups: European, Arab, African

- Major religious groups: Catholic, Anglican, Baptist, United Church of Christ

- Largest metropolitan areas in each province: Saint John, N.B., population 122,678; Halifax, N.S., 359,183 (13th-largest in Canada); Charlottetown, P.E.I., 58,358

- Other major cities: Fredericton and Moncton, N.B.; Truro, N.S.

- Life expectancy at birth, 3 year average 1995–1997: New Brunswick: men 74.8 years, women 81.2, total both sexes 78.0, ranking 5th among provinces and territories; Nova Scotia: men 74.8 years, women 80.6, total 77.7, 9th; Prince Edward Island: men 74.5 years, women 81.5, total 77.9, 6th; Canadian average: men 75.4, women 81.2, total 78.4

- Immigration 7/1/2000–6/30/2001: New Brunswick: 882, 0.3% of Canadian total of 252,088, ranking 8th among provinces and territories; Nova Scotia: 1,759, 0.7%, 7th; Prince Edward Island: 193, 0.08%, 10th

Plants and Animals

- Provincial flowers: New Brunswick: purple violet; Nova Scotia: mayflower; Prince Edward Island: Lady's Slipper (an orchid)

- Provincial trees: New Brunswick: balsam fir; Nova Scotia: red spruce; Prince Edward Island: red oak

- Endangered, threatened, or vulnerable species: more than fifty, including Atlantic whitefish, right whale, Blanding's turtle, lynx, ribbon snake, yellow lamp mussel, piping plover, roseate tern, and harlequin duck

Holidays

- National: January 1 (New Year's Day); Good Friday; Easter; Easter Monday; July 1 or, if this date falls on a Sunday, July 2 (Canada's birthday); 1st Monday of September (Labour Day); 2nd Monday of October (Thanksgiving); November 11 (Remembrance Day); December 25 (Christmas); December 26 (Boxing Day)

- Provincial: New Brunswick Day: 1st Monday in August; Nova Scotia: December 24 (half-day)

Economy

- Gross domestic product per capita: New Brunswick: $22,187 in 1999, ranking 11th among provinces and territories and 65.6% compared to U.S. average; Nova Scotia: $22,336, 10th, 66.0%; Prince Edward Island: $20,545, 13th, 60.7%[22]

- Major exports: building and construction products, paper and wood products, fish, processed foods and beverages

- Agriculture: potatoes, tobacco, dairy products, poultry, apples

- Mining: refined oil, coal, zinc, silver, lead, salt, gypsum

Notes

Introduction: Atlantic Canada

1. Harry Bruce, "Canadian Maritimes," *National Geographic Traveler.* www.nationalgeographic.com.

Chapter 1: Bound by the Sea

2. Mary Duenwald, "Puzzle of the Century," *Smithsonian,* January 2003. www.smithsonianmag.com

Chapter 2: Native Peoples and European Settlers

3. Quoted in "The Native People," Miramichi History, *Gateway Miramichi.* www.mibc.nb.ca.
4. David Stanley, *Canada's Maritime Provinces.* Victoria, Australia: Lonely Planet, 2002, p. 14.
5. Duenwald, "Puzzle of the Century."
6. Quoted in "History of Nova Scotia: Book #1, Acadia," History, *Blupete.* www.blupete.com.
7. Will Ferguson, "Mythic Isle," *Maclean's,* August 12, 2002. www.macleans.ca.
8. Ferguson, "Mythic Isle."

Chapter 3: Strength Through Diversity

9. *Western Valley Development Association,* "History and Overview of the Western Valley." www.wvda.com.
10. Fred McMahon, "A Sketch of Maritime Economic History," *Atlantic Institute for Market Studies.* www.aims.ca.
11. Ian Darragh, "Prince Edward Island: A World Apart No More," *National Geographic,* May 1998, p. 104.
12. Darragh, "Prince Edward Island," p. 104.

Chapter 4: Daily Life

13. Mark Morris, *Atlantic Canada Handbook*. Chico, CA: Moon, 1999, p. 178.

14. *Maclean's*, "Innovation with Lifestyle Attached," November 5, 2001. www.macleans.ca.

15. Mark Kurlansky, *Cod: A Biography of the Fish That Changed the World*. New York: Penguin, 1998, p. 128.

Chapter 5: Arts and Culture

16. James Ledbetter, "36 Hours: Prince Edward Island," *The New York Times*, August 16, 2002, p. F4.

17. Wayne Curtis et al., *Frommer's Canada*. New York: Macmillan, 1998, p. 43.

Chapter 6: Current Challenges

18. Bruce, "Canadian Maritimes."

19. Wayne C. Thompson, *Canada 2000*, 16th ed. Harper's Ferry, WV: Stryker-Post Publications, 2000, p. 87.

20. Demont, John, "No Longer McJobs," *Maclean's*, May 27, 2002. www.macleans.ca.

21. Patricia Harris, "Acadians Showcase a Heritage," *Boston Globe*, May 5, 2002, p. M9.

Facts About the Maritime Provinces

22. *Demographia*, "Canada: Regional Gross Domestic Product Data: 1999." www.demographia.com.

Chronology

B.C.

10,000   Evidence suggests that a native settlement exists on Prince Edward Island.

1000   The native village of Red Bank thrives on New Brunswick.

A.D.

circa 1000   Nova Scotia visited by the Norse.

1497   John Cabot claims Nova Scotia for the British.

1534   French explorer Jacques Cartier explores the coast of New Brunswick and also lands on Prince Edward Island.

1598   The French put forty convicts on Sable Island.

1604–1605   Pierre de Monts and Samuel de Champlain explore the coast of Nova Scotia and build the first French settlement in North America at Port Royal.

1621   The British king James I of England grants Acadia to William Alexander; he dubs it New Scotland (Nova Scotia).

1621   French signing of the Treaty of Utrecht gives Acadia and Nova Scotia (not including Cape Breton Island) to the British.

1719 The first French settlement on Prince Edward Island (which the French call "Ile Saint-Jean") occurs near present-day Charlottetown.

1751 The French build Fort Beauséjour to challenge British claims to Acadia.

1755 The British seize Fort Beauséjour and begin deportation of Acadians.

1763 Britain gains control of what they call Isle St. John through the Treaty of Paris and annex it to Nova Scotia.

1764 Britain allows exiled Acadians to return to Nova Scotia.

1769 Isle St. John becomes a separate colony.

1783 Seven thousand Loyalists land at Saint John.

1784 Britain makes New Brunswick, Nova Scotia, and Cape Breton Island separate colonies.

1789 First University in Canada founded, King's College in Halifax, Nova Scotia.

1799 The British rename Isle St. John "Prince Edward Island" after Edward, duke of Kent.

1820 Cape Breton Island is made a part of Nova Scotia.

1842 The border between Maine and New Brunswick is settled by the Webster-Ashburton Treaty.

1862 Mount Allison University in Sackville, N.B., becomes the first Canadian university to admit women as students.

1867 New Brunswick and Nova Scotia are two of the four original provinces in the founding of the confederation of Canada.

1873 Prince Edward Island joins the confederation.

1876   The Intercolonial Railway from New Brunswick to Montreal is completed.

1877   A massive fire in Saint John kills eighteen and leaves thirteen thousand homeless.

1917   Two ships collide in Halifax harbor, exploding 400,000 pounds of dynamite, killing two-thousand people, and destroying much of the harbor and downtown area.

1952   A major zinc-lead deposit is found near Bathurst, New Brunswick.

1959   Saint Lawrence Seaway opens.

1960   Louis Robichaud is elected as the first Acadian premier of New Brunswick.

1969   New Brunswick passes a language law making it the only officially bilingual province in Canada and recognizing the equality of English and French in the legislature, courts, and public service.

1969   Canada declares a 200-mile coastal fishing zone.

1997   The Confederation Bridge between New Brunswick and Prince Edward Island is completed.

1999   Natural gas production begins on Sable Island.

For Further Reading

Books

Charles Armour and Thomas Lackey, *Sailing Ships of the Maritimes.* Toronto: McGraw-Hill, 1975. This illustrated compilation of ships and stories includes numerous original documents and diary entries from maritime shippers and privateers during the region's shipping heyday.

Mark Morris, *Atlantic Canada Handbook.* Chico, CA: Moon, 1999. This useful guide presents broad historical overviews as well as details on the charms of the region.

Howard Norman, *How Glooskap Outwits the Ice Giants and Other Tales of the Maritime Indians.* Boston: Little, Brown, 1989. Compiled by a scholar who has studied and translated numerous Canadian native writings, this small book contains fascinating myths of the Mi'kmaq people.

Roger E. Riendeau, *A Brief History of Canada.* Allston, MA: Fitzhenry and Whiteside, 2000. A survey of Canada from its earliest inhabitants to national status to today's economy, with maps and illustrations.

David Stanley, *Canada's Maritime Provinces.* Victoria, Australia: Lonely Planet, 2002. Stanley's guide to the Maritime region gives succinct history and geographical information, then gives readers the best spots to visit in each province.

Periodicals

Ian Darragh, "Prince Edward Island: A World Apart No More," *National Geographic,* May 1998.

Websites

The Canadian Encyclopedia (www.thecanadianencyclopedia.com). This online encyclopedia is authoritative and comprehensive in scope.

The Government of New Brunswick (www.gnb.ca). Provides much factual background information as well as useful links.

The Government of Nova Scotia (www.gov.ns.ca). Offers everything from press releases to maps.

The Government of Prince Edward Island (www.gov.pe.ca). Provides information on the province's geography, culture, history, and more.

Works Consulted

Books

Wayne Curtis et al., *Frommer's Canada*. New York: Macmillan, 1998. One of the best overall travel guides to the country.

Trudy Fong, *Off the Beaten Path: The Maritime Provinces, A Guide to Unique Places,* 3d ed. Guilford, CT: Globe Pequot, 2001. Fong explores places one is unlikely to find readily in travel brochures.

Don Gillmor, Achille Michaud, and Pierre Turgeon, *Canada: A People's History*. Toronto: McClelland & Stewart, 2001. This two-volume family reference covers the beginnings of Canada to the 1990s.

Wilfred Kerr, *The Maritime Provinces of British North America and the American Revolution.* New York: Russell & Russell, 1971. This academic work discusses the process that led to the Loyalist migration during and after the American Revolution.

Mark Kurlansky, *Cod: A Biography of the Fish That Changed the World*. New York: Penguin, 1998. An interesting social history of a North Atlantic staple.

Stanley T. Spicer, *Masters of Sail: The Era of Square-Rigged Vessels in the Maritime Provinces.* Halifax: Petheric, 1968. Spicer describes the great vessels of the era as well as the lifestyles of the sailors.

Wayne C. Thompson, *Canada 2000*, 16th ed. Harper's Ferry, WV: Stryker-Post Publications, 2000. Provides concise summaries of Canada's geography, people, history, and culture.

Periodicals

Patricia Harris, "Acadians Showcase a Heritage," *Boston Globe*, May 5, 2002.

James Ledbetter, "36 Hours: Prince Edward Island," *The New York Times*, August 16, 2002.

Internet Sources

Blupete, History, "History of Nova Scotia: Book #1, Acadia." www.blupete.com.

Harry Bruce, "Canadian Maritimes," *National Geographic Traveler*. www.nationalgeographic.com.

Demographia, "Canada: Regional Gross Domestic Product Data: 1999." www.demographia.com.

Mary Duenwald, "Puzzle of the Century," *Smithsonian*, January 2003. www.smithsonianmag.com.

Gateway Miramichi, Miramichi History, "The Native People." www.mibc.nb.ca.

Fred McMahon, "A Sketch of Maritime Economic History," *Atlantic Institute for Market Studies*. www.aims.ca.

New Brunswick Community College Saint John, Heritage Resources, Saint John Historical Tour, "1860-1869." www.saintjohn.nbcc.nb.ca.

Wayne Thibodeau, "Elephantmania: Interest in a Rock Hits Fevered Pitch," *Elephant Rock*. www.elephantrock.org.

Western Valley Development Association, "History and Overview of the Western Valley." www.wvda.com.

Websites

Maclean's Magazine (www.macleans.ca). A valuable source of top-notch Canadian journalism.

Statistics Canada (www.statcan.ca). The Canadian census department's website offers diverse facts and figures on the country, provinces, and individual communities.

Index

Picture Credits

© Canadian Heritage Gallery/National Archives of Canada, 19, 27, 30, 33, 35, 37, 38, 42, 45, 47, 56, 65, 75

© Canadian National Railroad, 60

© Canadian Tourism Commission, 21, 22, 90, 91

© Cavendish Figurines, 76

© Council of Atlantic Premiers, 86

© Gilles Daigle/Images of New Brunswick, 92

© André Gallant/Images of New Brunswick, 64

© Halifax Regional Municipality, 68

© J. D. Richardson, 24

© National Archives of Canada, 39, 44, 49, 52, 69

© Carl & Ann Purcell/CORBIS, 84

© Reuters New Media Inc./CORBIS, 62

© Roger Lloyd for Sherbrooke Village & The Nova Scotia Museum, 79

© Saint John Theatre Co., 71

© John Sylvester/Tourism Prince Edward Island, 13, 16, 20, 53, 74, 93

© Tourism Saint John, 9, 57, 72

About the Authors

Gordon D. Laws graduated with a Bachelor of Arts in English from Brigham Young University. He is the author of several short stories, numerous magazine articles, and the novel *My People*. Currently, he is a freelance writer and editor. Lauren M. Laws graduated with a Bachelor of Arts in history from Brigham Young University. She is a researcher and records expert. In addition to this work, Gordon and Lauren collaborated on *Exploring Canada: Alberta* and *Exploring Canada: Manitoba*. Gordon and Lauren live in Massachusetts with their son, Grant.

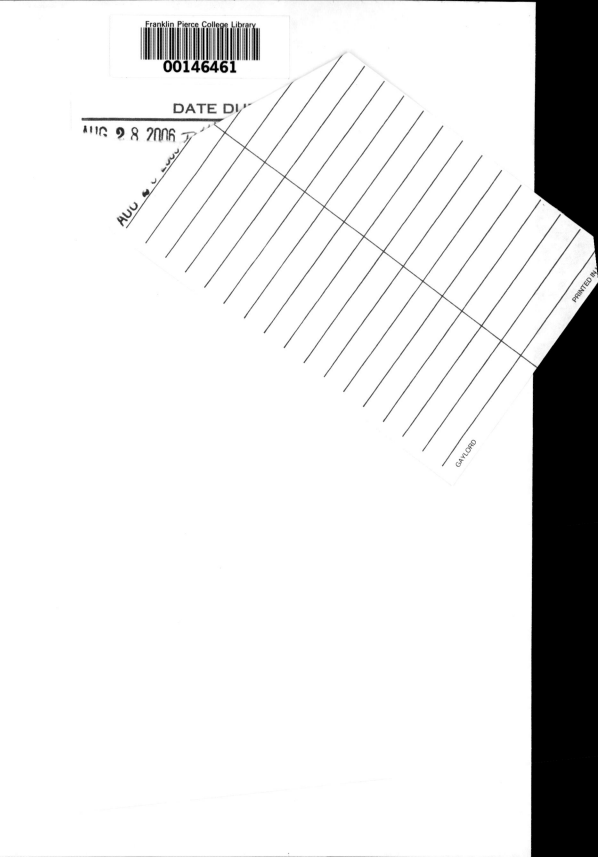